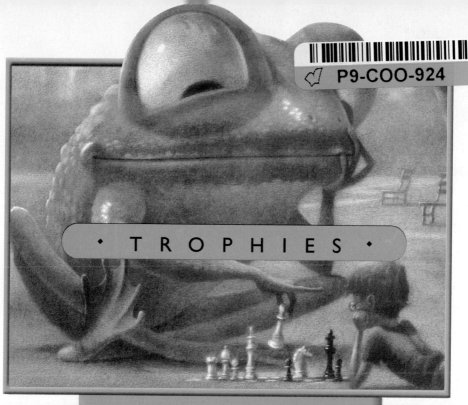

• T R O P H I E S •

Language Handbook

Grade 3

Copyright © by Harcourt, Inc.

Requests for permission to make copies of any part of the work should be addressed to School Permissions and Copyrights, Harcourt, Inc., 6277 Sea Harbor Drive, Orlando, Florida 32887-6777. Fax: 407-345-2418.

HARCOURT and the Harcourt Logo are trademarks of Harcourt, Inc., registered in the United States of America and/or other jurisdictions.

Printed in the United States of America

ISBN 0-15-325065-8

13 14 076 10 09 08 07 06 05

Orlando   Boston   Dallas   Chicago   San Diego

Visit *The Learning Site!*
www.harcourtschool.com

CONTENTS

Visit *The Learning Site!*
www.harcourtschool.com

Contents

contents

Your Best Writing

When you first learn a new game, such as tennis or baseball, you usually are not very good at it. The more you play, the better you can become.

You can also get better at writing by doing it. This handbook will give you the skills, strategies, tips, and models you need to become the best writer you can be.

The Writing Process

Writing is a process in which you try different things and go through different steps. The writing process is often divided into five stages. Most writers go back and forth through these stages.

Writing for Tests

When you write for a test, you usually don't have time for all the steps of the writing process. Here are some tips that can help you with test taking:

- Study the prompt carefully.
- Plan ahead.
- Keep track of the time.

For more about test taking, see pages 52–54. ➡

Prewriting

In this stage, you plan what you are going to write. You choose a topic and brainstorm ideas about it. You think of a good order for the ideas.

Drafting

In this stage, you put your ideas in writing as sentences and paragraphs. Follow your prewriting plan to write a first draft.

Revising

In this stage, you may work by yourself or with a partner or a group. Look over your writing, and see how you can make it clearer and stronger.

Proofreading

In this stage, you polish your work. Check for mistakes in grammar, spelling, capitalization, and punctuation. Make a final copy of your composition.

Publishing

Finally, you choose a way to present your work to others. You may want to add pictures, make a class book, or read your work aloud.

Keeping a Writer's Journal

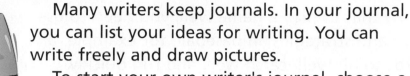

Many writers keep journals. In your journal, you can list your ideas for writing. You can write freely and draw pictures.

To start your own writer's journal, choose a notebook. Draw pictures on the cover. Then start filling the pages with your notes and ideas.

You may also want to keep a **Word Bank** at the back of your journal. Here you can list words to use in your writing. Make lists of different kinds of words, such as describing words, strong verbs, sports words, words about animals.

Keeping a Portfolio

A portfolio is a collection of a person's work. It may include samples of writing, drawings, and photographs.

Student writers often keep their main pieces of writing in a portfolio. You can choose the writing you want to put in your portfolio.

Use your portfolio when you have writing conferences with your teacher. A writing conference is the time to talk about your work. Tell what you are working on now. Set goals for yourself as a writer.

Reading ↔ Writing Connection

Written words are all around us. Pay attention to the words you see on television, in advertisements, and in books and magazines. When you spot an interesting word or phrase, write it in your Word Bank.

Writer's Craft

You know that to play a game well, you need to use special skills and strategies. In baseball, for example, a player needs to hit well, catch well, and run quickly.

Good writing takes special skills and strategies, too. This web shows the traits, or characteristics, of good writing. You will learn much more about these traits in this handbook.

The Traits of Good Writing

Conventions
Correct punctuation, grammar, spelling

Development
Reasons and details

Organization
Logical and clear order

Word Choice
Interesting verbs, adjectives, and nouns

Focus/Ideas
Interesting, clear content

Voice
Your own words and ideas

Effective Paragraphs
Each paragraph about one thing

Effective Sentences
Different kinds of sentences

Traits Checklist

As you practice writing, ask yourself these questions.

☑ **FOCUS/IDEAS**	Is my purpose clear? Do I stay on the topic?
☑ **ORGANIZATION**	Are my ideas in a clear order? Do I have a beginning, a middle, and an ending?
☑ **VOICE**	Do I use my own words and ideas? Do I seem to care about my topic and my audience?
☑ **WORD CHOICE**	Do I use specific nouns, strong verbs, and colorful adjectives?
☑ **DEVELOPMENT**	Do I use details to support my ideas?
☑ **EFFECTIVE SENTENCES**	Do I use different kinds of sentences?
☑ **EFFECTIVE PARAGRAPHS**	Are my ideas grouped in paragraphs? Do I use transitions such as time-order words?
☑ **CONVENTIONS**	Are my spelling, grammar, and punctuation correct?

Try This! Choose a piece of writing from your portfolio. Use the Traits Checklist. What are your strengths? How can you do better? Jot down your ideas in your Writer's Journal.

Focus/Ideas

Before you begin writing, you must choose a **focus**—the main idea or event you want to tell about. You may brainstorm many ideas before you choose one. You must also decide on your **purpose** for writing—for example, whether you want to entertain your readers with a story or inform them about an interesting topic. As you explain the main idea or event, remember to keep your focus and purpose in mind.

Read this student's paragraph that contrasts. Think about how the writer stays focused on the topic and purpose.

Student Model

Parakeets and macaws are different sizes and make different noises. Parakeets are small, slender birds. They are only 7 to 11 inches long. Macaws are very large birds. They can be 30 to 40 inches long. Parakeets can chirp loudly, but not as loudly as macaws. Macaws can make loud screeching noises to scare any animal that might want to eat them.

The first sentence tells the main idea.

The writer gives facts about size and then about sounds.

The writer sticks to the purpose of giving information.

How to Focus Your Writing

Strategies	Examples
• **Decide on a topic.**	• Tell the difference between parakeets and macaws.
• **Think of ideas about the topic.**	• Look in a book about birds. Go to a pet store or a zoo. Talk to a friend who has parakeets.
• **Keep your purpose in mind. Stay on the topic.**	• The purpose is to inform readers. • The topic sentence names two ways the birds are different. The other sentences give facts about the two differences.

Try This! Tell how you might get ideas for writing about each of these topics: **(1)** your favorite kind of pet, **(2)** the traits of a good teacher, **(3)** a space shuttle launch.

Reading ↔ Writing Connection

Think of your favorite story. What is the main point or idea of the story? What was the author's purpose for writing?

Focus/Ideas

Now it's your turn! Write a paragraph that is focused and interesting.

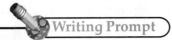

Writing Prompt

Think of a place you would like to visit. Find a book or an article about the place, some pictures of the place, and a map showing where it is. Then write a paragraph about why you would like to go there. Be sure to stay focused on your topic and main idea.

Strategies Good Writers Use

- Remember your audience and purpose.
- Support each point with interesting facts and details.

Prewrite

Make a web to plan your paragraph.

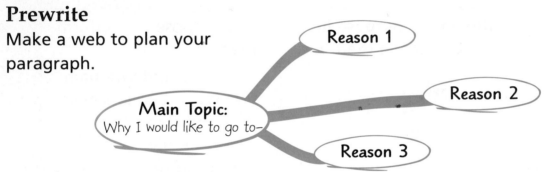

Reason 1

Reason 2

Main Topic:
Why I would like to go to—

Reason 3

Draft

Follow these steps:

STEP 1 **Introduce the topic.** Write a sentence that introduces the main topic.

STEP 2 **Organize the reasons.** Determine the order of your reasons.

STEP 3 **Add supporting facts and details.** Add facts and details to support each reason.

STEP 4 **Conclude with a summary.** Summarize your main idea in your last sentence.

Revise

Read over the draft of your paragraph. Use this checklist to help you revise your paragraph:

☑ Does your writing show your focus?

☑ Are your ideas well organized?

☑ Will your audience understand the purpose of your paragraph?

Proofread

Use this checklist as you proofread your paragraph:

☑ Do your sentences begin with capital letters?

☑ Have you used capital letters for the names of places?

☑ Have you checked your spelling?

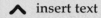	delete text
∧	insert text
↻	move text
¶	new paragraph
≡	capitalize
/	lowercase
○	correct spelling

Publish and Reflect

Make a final copy of your paragraph, and share it with a partner. Is there any information you don't understand? If so, talk about how to explain it better. Discuss how organizing information helps you focus on your purpose for writing. Take notes in your Writer's Journal.

Organization

Writers put ideas or events in an order that will make them easy to understand. The order of ideas or events is called **organization**. In a story, the events are usually in time order, or the order in which they happen. In writing that explains or informs (called expository writing), writers put their main points and details in an order that makes sense. An **outline** is helpful for expository writing because it shows how all the ideas in a piece of writing are related.

Read this student's outline and informative paragraph. Think about how the writer organizes information.

Student Model

Zebras

I. Size

   A. Smaller than most horses

   B. 4–5 feet high at shoulders

II. Appearance

   A. White with black stripes

   B. Short mane

   C. Large ears

Zebras are smaller than most horses. Most are four to five feet high at the shoulders. They have white coats with black stripes. Zebras' manes are short, but their ears are large.

What are the two main headings in this student's outline?

Details are identified by capital letters.

The ideas in the paragraph follow the same order as the outline.

How to Organize Information

1. Decide on your main points.

2. Put your points in an order that makes sense. Here are some frameworks that are often used to organize ideas:

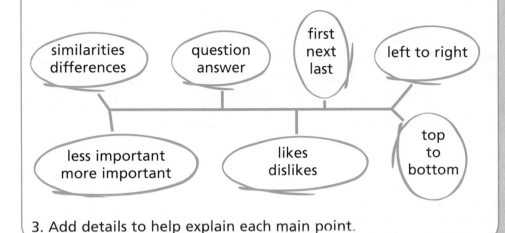

similarities
differences

question
answer

first
next
last

left to right

less important
more important

likes
dislikes

top
to
bottom

3. Add details to help explain each main point.

Try This! Look up an interesting subject in an encyclopedia. Make an outline of the article. Use your outline to make a brief oral report to the class.

Writing Forms

A research report begins with an interesting introduction, presents main points in an order that makes sense, and ends with a conclusion that summarizes the information.

For more about report writing, see pages 70–71.

Organizing Information

Now it's your turn! Write a research report that puts ideas in an order that makes sense.

Write a research report about a job that is important to the community. Begin with a paragraph that introduces your topic. Your report should include at least two main points with supporting details, as well as a concluding paragraph.

Strategies Good Writers Use

- Gather information.
- Decide on your main points.
- Include facts that will inform your audience about each main point.

Prewrite

Write down facts about the job. Then make an outline.

Draft

Follow these steps to help you organize your report:

Title of Outline (your topic)

I. Main point (one way job is important)
 A. Detail about the point
 B. Another detail

II. Main point (another way job is important)
 A. Detail about this point
 B. Another detail

STEP 1 **Introduce the topic** in the first paragraph.

STEP 2 **Organize the main points in an order that makes sense.** Decide how to order the main points you researched.

STEP 3 **Add supporting facts and details** to support each main point.

STEP 4 **End with a summary** in the last paragraph.

Revise

Read over the draft of your research report. Is there anything you would like to change or add? Use this checklist to revise your report:

☑ Does your writing have a clear purpose?

☑ Does each paragraph have a main idea?

☑ Is the information well organized?

Proofread

Use this checklist as you proofread your research report:

☑ Do your sentences begin with capital letters?

☑ Have you used commas and periods where they are needed?

☑ Have you indented paragraphs?

☑ Have you checked your spelling?

ℓ	delete text
∧	insert text
↪	move text
¶	new paragraph
≡	capitalize
/	lowercase
○	correct spelling

Publish and Reflect

Make a final copy of your report, and share it with a partner. Is there any information your partner doesn't understand? If so, talk about how to explain it better. Discuss how organizing information helps you carry out your purpose for writing. Write your ideas in your Writer's Journal.

Voice

You have your own special way of doing things. You have your own special way of saying things, too. The words you use and the way you put them together make your writing special.

The way in which you express yourself is called your **voice**. Your personal voice is what makes your writing interesting and lively. It shows how you feel about your topic and helps your readers to see things as you do.

Read this student's paragraph that describes a scene. Think about how the writer shows how he or she feels about the subject.

Student Model

Some large white birds were swimming on the pond. My dad said they were swans. I watched them skim silently across the water like skaters on ice. Their long necks curved gently from side to side. Suddenly there was a huge splash! The biggest swan rose up, beating the water with its enormous wings. I jumped, and then I laughed. Those swans weren't so gentle and quiet after all!

The writer compares the swans to skaters on ice.

What words does the writer use to describe the swan and its actions?

The writer expresses his or her feelings.

How to Develop Your Personal Voice

Strategies	How to Use the Strategies	Examples
• Use words that show how you see your subject.	• Use interesting words that help your reader picture the subject you are describing.	• Use words such as *skipped* or *tiptoed* instead of *went*. Use words such as *huge* or *giant* instead of *big*.
• Be honest, and express your own viewpoint.	• Let your reader know how you feel about the subject.	• If you think a lizard is ugly and scary, say so. If you think it is beautiful and fascinating, say so.

Try This! Practice writing a letter to a friend or relative. Try to write as if you are speaking to that person. Let your personal voice come through.

Writing Forms

A descriptive paragraph uses interesting words to help readers form pictures in their minds.

For more about descriptive writing, see page 58. ➡

Voice

Now it's your turn! Write a personal narrative using your own voice.

 **Writing Prompt**

Write a personal narrative about an activity you enjoy. Describe an event that happened when you did this activity. Then tell something that this event taught you about yourself. Organize your story so that it has a clear beginning, middle, and ending.

<blockquote>
Strategies Good Writers Use

- Decide what you want to show in your narrative.
- Use details that will help the reader share your experience.
</blockquote>

Prewrite

Make a web to plan your narrative.

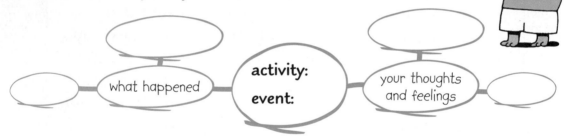

what happened

activity:

event:

your thoughts and feelings

Draft

Follow these steps:

STEP 1 **Begin by describing the activity**. Tell readers why you enjoy this activity.

STEP 2 **Express your viewpoint through details.** Describe something that happened when you did this activity.

STEP 3 **End by telling readers what you learned about yourself.**

Revise

Read over the draft of your personal narrative. Use this checklist to help you revise your narrative:

- ☑ Will your reader be able to picture the event?

- ☑ Can you use stronger words to describe the event?

- ☑ Did you express your viewpoint?

- ☑ Does your personal voice come through?

Proofread

Use this checklist as you proofread your narrative:

- ☑ Have you used correct capitalization and end marks?

- ☑ Have you checked to see that each sentence has a subject and a predicate?

- ☑ Have you checked your spelling?

ℒ	delete text
∧	insert text
↻	move text
¶	new paragraph
≡	capitalize
/	lowercase
◯	correct spelling

Publish and Reflect

Make a final copy of your personal narrative. Then read it to two of your classmates. Listen as they read their narratives. Think about the different ways the writers express their ideas. Discuss how you can make your voice stronger. Take notes in your Writer's Journal.

Word Choice

When you write, you should choose your words carefully. You want your ideas to be as clear and interesting as possible. You don't have to have a big vocabulary to write well. You already know many **strong verbs, specific nouns**, and **vivid describing words** that can make your writing better.

Read Teresa's persuasive letter. Think about what she wants Carmen to do and the words she chooses to express her ideas.

Student Model

Dear Carmen,

I found a photograph of a hairstyle that would look great on you. It's so pretty the way it ripples over the head and flares out just below the ears.

I imagine your hair swaying to the music as you dance. It would bounce and swing as you leap high and twirl around.

I am coming to your ballet recital next weekend. I'll see you there, and I hope I will see your new hairstyle, too!

Your friend,

Teresa

What does the writer want her friend to do?

Notice the vivid verbs that help you picture the actions.

Specific nouns make writing more interesting.

How to Choose Words

Strategies	How to Use the Strategies	Examples
• **Use strong verbs.**	• Choose verbs that describe actions clearly.	• A car **went** by. • A car **whizzed** by.
• **Use specific nouns.**	• Choose nouns that name one thing instead of nouns that name a whole group.	• The **food** was delicious. • The **spaghetti** was delicious.
• **Use vivid describing words.**	• Avoid words that are used too often.	• The new park has a **great** beach on a lake. • The new park has a **sandy** beach on a **sparkling blue** lake.

Try This! Write an advertisement for a lemonade stand. How can you persuade people to buy your lemonade? What strong words can you use to get customers' attention?

Reading ↔ Writing Connection

Find a piece of persuasive writing in a magazine or newspaper. Choose several words that help state the writer's opinions. Add them to your Word Bank.

Word Choice

Now it's your turn! Write a persuasive paragraph. Use strong and specific words to persuade readers to agree with you.

Writing Prompt

Write a paragraph that persuades your classmates that regular practice will help them improve a skill. State your opinion. Then give reasons that support your opinion. Finally, encourage your classmates to take action.

Strategies Good Writers Use

- Decide on your purpose and audience.
- Think of reasons and details that will persuade your readers to share your opinion.

Prewrite

Use a chart to plan your paragraph.

My Opinion:	
Reason:	Details:
Reason:	Details:
Action requested:	

Draft

Follow these steps to help you organize your paragraph:

STEP 1 **Get your audience's attention.** Write a strong statement of opinion.

STEP 2 **State your reasons.** Write at least two reasons that support your opinion. Add details to make each reason clear.

STEP 3 **Call your readers to action.** Restate your opinion. Then urge your readers to take action.

Revise

Read your persuasive paragraph. Use this checklist to help you revise your writing:

- ☑ Have you made it clear what you want your reader to do?

- ☑ Have you given good reasons to persuade your reader?

- ☑ Did you use strong verbs and specific nouns?

Proofread

Use this checklist as you proofread your paragraph:

- ☑ Does each sentence begin with a capital letter?

- ☑ Have you used the correct end marks?

- ☑ Have you used a dictionary to check your spelling?

ℓ	delete text
^	insert text
↻	move text
¶	new paragraph
≡	capitalize
/	lowercase
○	correct spelling

Publish and Reflect

Exchange paragraphs with a partner. Share ideas about how word choice can improve your persuasive writing. Write your ideas in your Writer's Journal.

Development

The way a writer explains or describes main ideas makes writing interesting. Using details to explain or describe is called **development.**

Development is important in all kinds of writing. In expository writing, facts, reasons, and examples are used to develop main ideas. In expressive writing, details that describe people, places, events, and feelings are important. Details help you paint a picture in your reader's mind or make a character come alive.

Read this student's description of a character. Think about how the details make the character seem real.

Student Model

The first time I met my mother's Aunt Jessie, I didn't know what to think of her. Aunt Jessie is as thin as a stick. She frowned at me and muttered, "So you're Paul, are you?"

"Yes, Aunt Jessie," I replied politely.

Suddenly she let out a lion's roar of a laugh. "We're going to be great friends, Paul," she declared.

I didn't know it then, but Aunt Jessie was right.

Why does the writer use "thin as a stick" rather than just "thin"?

What detail helps you imagine the laugh?

How do you think the writer feels about Aunt Jessie?

How to Develop Ideas

Strategies	How to Use the Strategies	Examples
• **Use specific details.**	• Details include facts, examples, descriptions, and dialogue.	• My favorite day of the week is Saturday. One reason is that I don't have to wake up to the loud buzz of my alarm clock.
• **Use words that show rather than tell.**	• Use words that help readers see, hear, feel, smell, or taste your subject.	• The boy's teeth chattered, and his face turned white.

Try This! Find a picture of an interesting-looking person in a magazine or newspaper. Paste the picture on a sheet of paper. Then write a description of the person. Use specific details to make your reader see the person in a certain way.

Reading ↔ Writing Connection

Find two stories in which the authors describe characters. Choose interesting words from the descriptions to add to your Word Bank.

Development

Now it's your turn! Write a story in which you develop a main character.

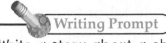

Writing Prompt

Write a story about a character who leaves a familiar place and travels to a new place, where he or she meets strangers and solves a problem.

Strategies Good Writers Use

- Think of an experience you have had that is like the one you are writing about.
- Picture in your mind the main character and events in your story.

Prewrite

Use a web to organize your ideas.

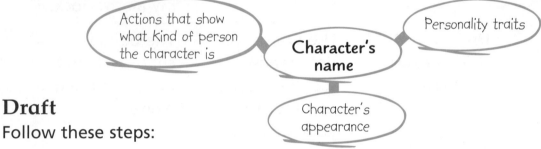

Actions that show what kind of person the character is

Personality traits

Character's name

Character's appearance

Draft

Follow these steps:

STEP 1 **Get your audience's attention.** Write a beginning that will interest your readers.

STEP 2 **Give the events in time order.** Tell the events in the order in which they happen.

STEP 3 **Solve the problem.** Have the character figure out a way to solve the problem.

Revise

Reread the draft of your story. Use this checklist to help you revise your work:

- ☑ Do you give your reader a clear picture of the character?
- ☑ Can you add details to describe the character better?
- ☑ Does your story have a beginning, a middle, and an ending?

Proofread

Use this checklist as you proofread your story:

- ☑ Does each sentence begin with a capital letter?
- ☑ Have you used the correct end marks?
- ☑ Have you used commas and quotation marks correctly?

ℓ	delete text
∧	insert text
↺	move text
¶	new paragraph
≡	capitalize
/	lowercase
○	correct spelling

Publish and Reflect

Make a final copy of your story. Share it with a partner. Discuss how you can develop the characters and events in other stories you might write. Make notes in your Writer's Journal.

Effective Sentences

Good writers use complete sentences that have clear subjects and predicates. Good writers also use different kinds of sentences. Some are short, and some are long. Some are statements, and some may be questions or exclamations. When you vary your sentences, your writing is more interesting.

This student's paragraph gives information by comparing two things. Think about the different kinds of sentences the writer uses to make the information clear and interesting.

Student Model

Horses and cows are a lot alike. They are both raised on either farms or ranches. Both are quite large, and they like to eat grass.

Horses and cows are important to humans, too. We get milk from cows, and we can ride horses. Can you think of other ways they are alike?

The writer starts with a simple statement.

A mix of long and short sentences makes the paragraph interesting to read.

The question adds variety.

How to Write Effective Sentences

Strategies	How to Use the Strategies
• **Write different kinds of sentences.**	• Don't make all your sentences alike. Use long sentences and short sentences. Use different kinds of sentences— statements, questions, and exclamations.
• **Combine sentences.**	• Look for places where you can use compound subjects and compound predicates. Combine simple sentences to write compound sentences.

Try This! Find two science articles on the same topic or on similar topics. Find one in your textbook and the other in a magazine or newspaper. Which article do you think uses more effective sentences? Why do you think so? Support your answer with reasons and examples.

Reading ↔ Writing Connection

Find a book of proverbs or famous quotations. Choose a proverb or quotation that you think is an especially effective sentence. Copy it into your Writer's Journal.

Effective Sentences

Now it's your turn! Write an essay that uses a variety of sentences to keep readers interested.

Writing Prompt

Write an essay for your classmates telling what you like and dislike about a season of the year. Use details and examples to explain your ideas.

Strategies Good Writers Use

- Brainstorm likes and dislikes.
- Think about details that you can use to explain your ideas.

Prewrite

Create a chart to organize your ideas.

Season:	
Likes	Dislikes
1.	1.
2.	2.

Draft

Follow these steps:

STEP 1 **Get your readers interested.** Make the opening interesting.

STEP 2 **Organize your essay.** Put the likes in one paragraph and the dislikes in another.

STEP 3 **Use details.** Explain each idea with examples from your own experience.

STEP 4 **Finish with a summary of your thoughts.** Tell whether your likes or your dislikes are stronger.

Revise

Reread the draft of your essay. Use this checklist to help you revise it:

☑ Will your reader understand how you feel about the season?

☑ Can you add details or examples to explain your likes or dislikes?

☑ Are all your sentences complete? Have you used different types of sentences?

Proofread

Use this checklist as you proofread your essay:

☑ Does each sentence begin with a capital letter?

☑ Have you used the correct end marks?

☑ Have you indented your paragraphs?

ℓ	delete text
∧	insert text
↪	move text
¶	new paragraph
☰	capitalize
/	lowercase
◯	correct spelling

Publish and Reflect

Make a final copy of your essay. Then share it with a partner. Tell your partner which sentences are effective and why. Write your reflections in your Writer's Journal.

Effective Paragraphs

Good writers organize their ideas and information into **paragraphs**. Writing good paragraphs makes what you have to say easy for a reader to understand. A paragraph usually has a topic sentence that states the main idea. The other sentences in the paragraph give details about the main idea.

Read this student's directions for making a garden sculpture. Think about how the writer makes the paragraph effective.

Student Model

Making a garden sculpture is fun and easy. First, take a clay saucer, the kind used under flowerpots. Use crayons to decorate the outside of the saucer. Then, fill it about three-fourths of the way with potting soil. Spray the soil with water to make it moist. Next, sprinkle on a layer of grass seed. Cover the seeds with a thin layer of soil, and spray again with water. Place the saucer in a sunny window. Once a day, spray the soil with water. After the grass sprouts, you can add decorations, such as twigs, pebbles, shells, or small toys.

The first sentence tells what this paragraph is about.

Time-order words such as *first*, *then*, and *next* make the sequence of steps clear.

All the sentences tell about the main idea.

How to Write Effective Paragraphs

Strategies	Applying the Strategies	Examples
• **Identify your topic.**	• Write a **topic sentence** that states the main idea.	• Making a garden sculpture is fun and easy.
• **Include details.**	• Give **details** about the main idea in other sentences.	• Use crayons to decorate the outside of the saucer.
• **Use sequence words.**	• Use time-order words such as *first*, *next*, and *last* to show the order of steps or events.	• *First*, take a clay saucer, the kind used under flowerpots.

Try This! Write directions for a simple activity, such as putting on your coat or washing your hands. Exchange directions with a classmate. Can your classmate follow your directions? Why or why not?

Reading ↔ Writing Connection

Find two writings that explain how to do something. Which one explains the topic more clearly? Support your answer with examples and details.

Effective Paragraphs

Now it's your turn to write a how-to paragraph!

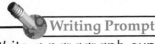

(**Writing Prompt**)

Write a paragraph explaining to your classmates how to do an activity that you do well. Tell what materials are needed. Then describe each step, using sequence words.

Prewrite

Write the main steps of the process in a flowchart. Add boxes as needed.

| Topic: |
| Materials needed: |

| Step 1 | | Step 2 | | Step 3 |

Draft

Follow these steps:

STEP 1 **Write a topic sentence.** Introduce the main idea.

STEP 2 **List materials.** Name all the materials needed.

STEP 3 **Describe each step.** Present specific details that describe each step clearly.

STEP 4 **Use sequence words.** Use words such as *first*, *next*, and *last* to show the correct order of steps.

Revise

Read over your draft. Use this checklist to help you revise your paragraph:

☑ Does your paragraph have an interesting topic sentence?

☑ Are any steps missing or out of order?

☑ Did you use sequence words?

☑ Are the detail sentences about the topic?

Proofread

Use this checklist to proofread your directions:

☑ Have you used capitalization and punctuation correctly?

☑ Have you used commands correctly?

☑ Have you used a dictionary to check your spelling?

ℓ	delete text
∧	insert text
↺	move text
¶	new paragraph
≡	capitalize
/	lowercase
○	correct spelling

Publish and Reflect

Make a final copy of your paragraph, and share it with a partner. Tell whether you think your partner's directions are clear. In your Writer's Journal, tell what you have learned about effective paragraphs.

Conventions

Our language follows **conventions**, or rules. We write in sentences. We end them with punctuation marks. We leave spaces between words, and we indent paragraphs. All of these conventions help readers make sense of writing.

As you proofread your writing, you check to make sure you have followed the conventions. These strategies can help you proofread:

How to Proofread

Wait before proofreading.
Put your writing away for a while. Then come back to it. You may see new things.

Proofread in steps.
1. Look at your **sentences**. Are they complete? Are they written correctly? Are your **paragraphs** indented?

2. Check your **language use**. Do your subjects agree with your verbs? Have you used the correct forms of adjectives and adverbs? Have you followed the rules for **capitalization** and **punctuation**?

3. Last, check your **spelling**. Circle any words that look strange. Use a dictionary if necessary.

Proofread with a partner.
Two pairs of eyes are better than one. Your classmate may find mistakes you did not see.

Proofreading Checklist

Sentences and Paragraphs

☑ Is every sentence complete?

☑ Does each sentence begin with a capital letter and end with the correct end mark?

☑ Is each paragraph indented?

Grammar and Usage

☑ Do your verbs agree with their subjects?

☑ Have you used the correct verb tenses?

☑ Have you used *I* and *me* correctly?

☑ Have you used the correct form of adjectives and adverbs that compare?

Capitalization and Punctuation

☑ Have you capitalized proper nouns?

☑ Have you used commas, quotation marks, and apostrophes correctly?

Spelling

☑ Are you sure of the spelling of every word?

☑ Have you always used *their* and *there* correctly?

☑ Have you spelled plural nouns correctly?

 ## Technology

If you use a computer spell checker, remember that it cannot tell homophones apart. For example, the spell checker does not know whether you mean *here* or *hear*.

Presenting Your Work

Sometimes you write for yourself. Most of the time, you write for other people. When you let other people read or hear your writing, you **publish** your work.

You can publish your writing in many ways. Here are some ideas.

Publishing Ideas for Any Type of Writing

- Read your writing aloud.

- Have a friend read it silently.

- Post it on a bulletin board.

Publishing Ideas for Descriptions and Poems

- Draw or paint a picture to go with your writing.

- Cut pictures from a magazine. Make a collage.

- Make up a dance to go with your writing.

- Find a piece of music to go with your writing. Make a tape recording in which you read while the music plays in the background.

Publishing Ideas for Stories

- Work with friends. Act out your story.
- Draw pictures to go with your story.
- Read your story aloud to another class.
- Make a class storybook.
- Send your story to a magazine.
- Mail your story to a relative far away.

Acting Out a Story

You can follow these steps to perform a story or a personal narrative.

Technology

You can use the computer to make a neat copy of your work. Type the words the way you wrote them. Use *Return* and then *Tab* to start a new paragraph.

STEP 1 Plan how the people in your story should sound to the audience. What are their voices like? How do they say their words? Experiment with your voice.

STEP 2 Find props for your story. You can use different kinds of clothing, pictures, and other items.

STEP 3 Decide how you want to present your story. Do you want to read it just as it is written, or do you want to act it out? You could even ask classmates to help you present your story as a play.

Publishing Ideas for Reports

- Add maps or pictures. Make a tabletop display.

- Make a poster for the classroom bulletin board.

- Teach your classmates about your topic.

- Put your report in the classroom library for others to read.

Publishing Ideas for Persuasive Writing

- Send a letter to the editor of your school paper.

- Give a speech to your class.

- Publish your ideas on your school's website.

- Read your work aloud. Take a poll. Find out who agrees with you.

Strategies Good Writers Use

- Give your work a title.
- Put your name on your work.
- Check your facts and proofread carefully before you send a letter in the mail or post work on a website.

Giving an Oral Report

Strategies	Applying the Strategies
Make notecards.	Write each main idea on a notecard. Number the notecards in order.
Practice.	Give your talk to a friend or family member. Think about how to make your talk better.
Speak clearly and slowly.	Speak more slowly than you do when you are just talking. Look at your audience. Remember that they can learn from you.

Strategies for Listeners

- Think about the speaker's main idea.
- Try to learn from what you hear.
- Ask questions to learn more.

Uppercase and Lowercase Manuscript Alphabet

Uppercase and Lowercase
Cursive Alphabet

A B C D E F G

H I J K L M N

O P 2 R S T

U V W X Y Z

a b c d e f g

h i j k l m n

o p q r s t

u v w x y z

D'Nealian
Manuscript Alphabet

A B C D E F G

H I J K L M N

O P Q R S T

U V W X Y Z

a b c d e f g

h i j k l m n

o p q r s t

u v w x y z

D'Nealian
Cursive Alphabet

A B C D E F G H

I J K L M N O P

2 R S T U V W

X Y Z

a b c d e f g h

i j k l m n o

p q r s t u v

w x y z

Elements of Handwriting

Shape

Make each letter the correct shape.

correct

Tuesday

incorrect

Tuesday

Spacing

Leave the correct amount of space between letters.
Leave one pencil space between words and after
end punctuation.

We ate pears.

Position and Size

Write all letters so they sit on the bottom line. Short letters should touch both the midline and the bottom line.

correct	incorrect
coat	*coat*

Slant

Slant your letters in the same direction. If you slant your paper correctly, it will help you slant your letters.

correct	incorrect
kite	*kite*

Stroke

When you write, keep your letter strokes smooth and even. The letters should not be too light or too dark.

correct	too light	too dark
car	*car*	*car*

Spelling Strategies

Does spelling seem easy or hard to you? Good spellers notice new words as they read and listen. They use their eyes and ears as they spell new words. Follow these steps to learn to spell a new word:

STEP 1 **Say the word.** Think: Where have you heard the word? How many syllables does the word have? What does it mean?

STEP 2 **Look at the word.** Find prefixes and suffixes that you know. Think: Do you know any other words that look like this?

STEP 3 **Spell the word to yourself.** Think about the way each sound is spelled. Try to picture the word in your mind.

STEP 4 **Write the word while looking at it.** Check your handwriting. If the word is not neat and clear, write it again.

STEP 5 **Check your learning.** Cover the word and write it. Did you spell the word correctly? If not, go back to step 1. Start again.

Making a Personal Spelling List

You may want to make a place in your Writer's Journal for a personal spelling list. This is where you can list words that you use often and words that are tricky for you. Before you begin, make columns on your pages for the letters of the alphabet. That way you can find words easily.

Follow these steps to make and use your personal spelling list.

1. Read your writing. Circle any word that you think may be misspelled.

2. Find out how to spell the word correctly. Use a dictionary, or ask someone.

3. Write the word in the spelling list in your journal. Also write its meaning, or use it in a sentence.

4. Use your spelling list to check your spelling as you proofread your writing.

Reading ↔ Writing Connection

As you read, add to your journal words you want to learn to spell. Use a dictionary to find their meaning. Practice spelling the new words. Then use them in your writing.

Peer Conferences

In a **peer conference**, students share their writing. Other students listen and respond. Peer conferences help writers get ideas about making their work more interesting and exciting.

How to Speak During a Peer Conference

Strategies for Speakers	Applying the Strategies
• **Read your work aloud.**	• Speak slowly and clearly. • Have a classmate read your work aloud. When you listen to your own writing, you may hear things that need to be fixed.
• **Respond to the work of others.**	• Tell exactly what you like and why. Tell what doesn't work and why. • Be polite. Don't say anything you wouldn't want to hear yourself. • Your classmates may like their writing as it is. There's no rule that says a writer must use your ideas.

How to Listen During a Peer Conference

Strategies for Listeners	Applying the Strategies
• **Be an active listener.**	• Pay attention. Don't talk, laugh, or move around. Think about the writer's main idea.
• **Take notes.**	• Write your questions or ideas about the writing you hear. • Take notes on your classmates' ideas about your writing.
• **Keep an open mind.**	• Don't be angry if your classmates have trouble understanding your writing. Think about what you could do to help them understand. • As your classmates read their work, don't think, "I could have written it better." Remember, every writer has his or her own voice and opinion.

Reading ↔ Writing Connection

As you read your classmates' writing, look for ideas you might use to make your own writing better.

Using Rubrics

Your teacher uses a **rubric**, or checklist, to give your writing a grade. The best writing has each of the traits on the rubric. Scores usually go from 1 to 4 points or from 1 to 6 points. Only the best writing earns the highest score.

Here is how you can use rubrics to make sure your writing is the best it can be.

Before Writing

• Review the checklist to find out what traits your writing should have.

• Think about these traits as you plan your writing.

During Writing

• Check your draft against the list to see if it is missing any key traits.

• On the checklist, put a mark next to each trait that is missing or can be improved.

• Use the marked list as you revise your draft.

After Writing

• Check your finished work against the list.

• Make sure your writing covers all the key points.

• If necessary, revise your draft again. Make another finished copy.

Strategies Good Writers Use

• Be sure you have done what the prompt asks you to do.

• Proofread carefully. Use a dictionary and your Language Handbook to check for spelling and grammar errors.

• Write neatly.

Some rubrics show only the highest score. Here is a rubric for a personal narrative. The highest score is 6 points.

SCORE OF 6 ★★★★★★

★ The story fits the purpose for writing. The story reaches its intended audience. The ideas are interesting.

★ The story has a clever beginning that tells the problem, a middle that tells events in order, and an ending that gives the solution to the problem.

★ The story has descriptive and rich details that help the reader visualize the events.

★ The story has interesting words and phrases, such as specific nouns, vivid verbs, sensory words, and comparisons. It shows the writer's feelings.

★ The sentences are written in a variety of ways and are interesting to read.

★ The story has few errors in spelling, grammar, and punctuation.

Writing for Tests

On some tests, you write about a topic that is given to you. You usually have a certain amount of time to complete the writing test.

A **prompt** tells you the topic of your writing. It may also tell you the purpose and form of your writing. To do well on the test, you must do what the prompt tells you to do.

Sample Writing Prompts

Everyone has a special place. Think of a place that is special to you. Now write about your special place.

Everyone enjoys playing or watching some kinds of games or sports. Think about a game or sport you enjoy. Now explain why you like that game or sport.

Everyone has special memories. Think about a time that was special to you. Now write a story that tells what happened during that time.

This sentence introduces the topic.

The next sentence gives an idea for prewriting. The third sentence tells you what to write about.

Looking for Clue Words

Sometimes a prompt has special words that tell you what or how to write. For example, a prompt might say, "write a letter to your teacher." This tells you that the form of your writing should be a letter. It also tells you that your audience is your teacher. You can also look for clue words that tell you whether you are writing to tell a story, to explain something, or to persuade.

Types of Writing Found on Tests

Type of Writing	Purpose	Clue Words in the Prompt
narrative	to tell a story	tell a story, tell about a time, tell what happened when
expository	to explain	explain why, tell how, explain how you would
persuasive	to persuade	persuade, convince, tell why you think, explain why you would

Writing for Tests

On a test, you have only a short time to write. Most tests expect you to prewrite, draft, and edit your work. You need time to do each of these steps.

Your teacher will tell you how much time you have for a writing test. For a test that is 45 minutes long, you might spend 10 minutes prewriting, 25 minutes drafting, and 10 minutes editing.

Tips for Managing Your Time

STEP 1 **Prewrite**
- Jot down your topic and form.
- List ideas, draw pictures, or make notes.

STEP 2 **Draft**
- Use your prewriting notes to write a draft.
- Check the prompt. Make sure you have done what it asked you to do.

STEP 3 **Edit (Revise and Proofread)**
- Add missing details.
- Take out details that don't support your main idea.
- Check your punctuation, capitalization, grammar, and spelling.

Writing Models

Story

In a **story**, a writer tells about one main idea. A *story* has *characters*, a *plot*, and a *setting*. It also has a *beginning*, a *middle*, and an *ending*.

Little Mouse Bells the Cat

title

The attic mice were all good friends, but they lived in fear of Claws, the house cat. Many mice had damaged tails because of Claws.

"If only we could hear him coming, we'd have time to run away," said Little Mouse.

The opening paragraphs set up the problem.

"We once had a plan to put a bell around his neck," said Bent-Tail.

"That's a great idea," cried Little Mouse. "Why didn't you do it?"

"I bent my tail trying," said Bent-Tail.

Just then, Knotted-Tail ran in.

"That cat took my cheese!" he cried.

Suddenly, Little Mouse had an idea. She ran to her nest, where she had hidden a bell. She slipped it onto a piece of ribbon. Then she put it on and went downstairs.

Claws heard her coming. "What's making that lovely noise?" he asked.

"It's my wonderful new necklace," squeaked Little Mouse.

"I want it," hissed the cat. "Give it to me, now!"

"Take it!" yelled Little Mouse, as she yanked off the necklace and ran away.

Claws put on his new necklace. He purred when he heard the lovely noise. From that day on, the mice could hear Claws coming.

The last paragraph solves the problem.

Descriptive Paragraph

A **descriptive paragraph** paints a word picture. It describes a person, a place, an object, or an event.

> Last fall, the air was <u>crisp</u> and <u>cool</u> as Sam and his big brother, Jerry, waited for the parade to pass. Suddenly, they heard the <u>thump</u> of the <u>big</u> school drum. The parade was coming! Jerry is tall, but even he had trouble seeing over all the people. Beside Jerry a <u>little</u> girl with a <u>sweet-smelling jelly</u> doughnut was crying. She couldn't see a thing. Jerry put her on his shoulders. Then she could see all the <u>high-stepping</u> marchers. The little girl <u>squealed</u> with delight!

topic sentence

detail sentences

Words that appeal to the senses make the writing come alive.

Character Sketch

In a **character sketch**, a writer describes a real or an imaginary person.

In the book <u>The Best Fall</u>, Jerry Adams is a tall but shy student at Midvale School and Sam's big brother. It isn't easy for Jerry to decide between the school band and the football team. Jerry chooses the school band, but he really wants to be a part of football, too. Jerry solves his problem in a clever way. Every Saturday, he helps coach Sam and the other third-graders on the little league football team. Jerry is one of the **kindest and smartest characters** in the whole book.

The topic sentence introduces the main character.

The writer uses a variety of sentences to tell how the character acts.

special qualities

Personal Narrative

In a **personal narrative**, a writer tells about an experience in his or her life.

Why was I named Cameroon Pelée? I never thought about it until a friend asked how I had gotten my name. I didn't know, so I went home to search for answers. First, I sat down to think. Then my sister Helen came in. She was born on the day a volcano named Mount Saint Helens erupted. That's how she got her name. I asked her how I had gotten mine. She said that I got my name the same way she did. It's true. I looked it up. I was born on the same day a volcano erupted in Cameroon, Africa.

The first sentence grabs the reader's attention.

Sequence words put events in time order.

ending

Paragraph of Information

A **paragraph of information** gives facts about one topic. It has a topic sentence that tells the main idea. At least two detail sentences give facts about the main idea.

The Peak of Perfection

Mount Cameroon is a special mountain in Africa. It is the highest mountain in western Africa and an active volcano. The last time Mount Cameroon erupted was over 30 years ago. Ash that came out of the volcano turned into rich soil. Farmers now grow tea, rubber trees, and cocoa in that soil. Mount Cameroon is also special because it is one of the wettest places on earth. More than 400 inches of rain fall there each year.

title

topic sentence

facts

Details all relate directly to the topic sentence.

How-to Paragraph

A **how-to paragraph** gives directions or explains how to do something. Steps are given in time order.

How to Make a Volcano

You can make a small volcano at home with an adult's help. You will need a pan, a plastic bottle, red food coloring, a bottle of vinegar, baking soda, and some sand. First, add a few drops of food coloring to the vinegar. Next, fill the plastic bottle halfway with baking soda and place it in the middle of the pan. Pile the sand around the bottle. Finally, ask the adult to quickly pour the vinegar into the hole. Stand back, and watch the volcano erupt.

topic sentence

Sequence words (underlined here) put the steps in time order.

Paragraph That Compares

In a **paragraph that compares,** a writer shows how people, places, or things are alike.

My sister Helen and I are alike in many ways. Both of us have curly black hair and brown eyes. We also share a sense of humor and enjoy telling jokes and stories to our friends. What makes us most alike is the way we got our names. Both Helen and I were named after volcanoes that erupted on the day we were born!

topic sentence

Each detail sentence names a way in which they are alike.

Paragraph That Contrasts

In a **paragraph that contrasts**, a writer shows how people, places, or things are different.

My sister Helen and I are different in a couple of ways. First, she is already in high school. Her school experience is helpful when she helps me figure out a tough class assignment. Another difference is that I always know where all our things are, but she always loses things. I don't know how Helen could find anything at all without me.

topic sentence

Detail sentences offer clear examples of the ways in which the people are different.

Persuasive Paragraph

In a **persuasive paragraph,** a writer tries to make readers agree with his or her opinion.

Whale-watching is good for people and for the environment. Many people have begun working for earth-friendly causes after sailing near whales. Also, these intelligent animals seem to like the visitors. Tourists describe excitedly how whales come up to the boats to be touched. Most important, whale-watching helps people learn how valuable and beautiful these mysterious mammals are. Everyone is helped by a whale-watching trip. Find out more about one today!

opinion in topic sentence

reasons and facts

The writer saves the strongest reason for last.

restated opinion or call for action

Summary

A **summary** helps the writer remember main points. A summary can be about information from a book, an article, a film, a talk, or something you observe. It is written in your own words. A summary has a main idea and a few important details.

> *Hamster* is the common name for any of 14 species of rodents. These animals have cheek pouches that they use to hold and carry large amounts of food. They also have thick fur and short tails. Hamsters are nocturnal, or active at night. They are desert animals and dig burrows with several compartments. Hamsters are mostly vegetarians. Their favorite foods include fruits, seeds, and green vegetation.
>
> The golden hamster from Syria and the dwarf hamster from Asia make excellent house pets that are easy to care for. They should be kept in wire, glass, or plastic cages. The floor of the cage should be lined with cedar shavings that are changed often. Hamsters need fresh water daily.

sample source article

Specially made water bottles can supply the water they need. Expect a pet hamster to live about three or four years.

Hamsters are rodents. They have thick fur, short tails, and cheek pouches to carry food. They are active at night and are mostly vegetarians.

Hamsters make good pets. Keep them in a cage with cedar shavings and fresh water.

summary

The writer uses his or her own words.

Response to Literature

A **book review** is a response to literature. It tells briefly what a book is about, without telling the ending. It also gives the writer's opinion of the book. Finally, it says whether others should read it.

When you write in response to literature, remember these tips:

- **Show your understanding of the work.**
- **Discuss literary elements such as characters, setting, plot, and main idea and details.**
- **Support your ideas and opinions with specific examples from the literature.**

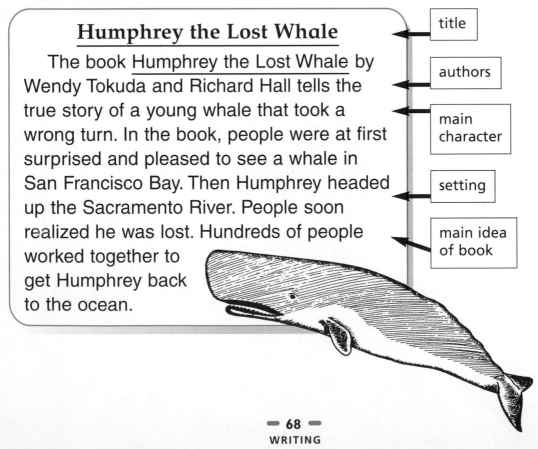

Humphrey the Lost Whale

The book Humphrey the Lost Whale by Wendy Tokuda and Richard Hall tells the true story of a young whale that took a wrong turn. In the book, people were at first surprised and pleased to see a whale in San Francisco Bay. Then Humphrey headed up the Sacramento River. People soon realized he was lost. Hundreds of people worked together to get Humphrey back to the ocean.

title

authors

main character

setting

main idea of book

This story is both exciting and educational. I learned a lot about whales as I read it. The pictures are beautiful, and the story will make you cheer.

I think that anyone who likes a good animal story with a lot of suspense should try Humphrey the Lost Whale. If you didn't know this was a true story, you would not believe it!

The writer gives reasons to support his or her opinion.

Research Report

To write a **research report**, a writer gathers facts from several sources, takes notes, and makes an **outline**. The notes and outline are used to write the report. The writer lists the sources at the end of the report.

Outline

An outline follows a certain form. Roman numerals show the main ideas. Letters show the subtopics.

**Scientists Predict
Volcanic Eruptions**

I. Information studied

   A. Volcano's history

   B. Rising ground

   C. Gases in the air

II. Kinds of warnings

   A. Before eruption

   B. Volcano drills

Research Report

A research report gives facts about a topic. This short report follows the outline on page 70. Reports can be several pages long.

Scientists Predict Volcanic Eruptions ← title

Scientists are getting better at telling when a volcano will erupt. ← main topic
One way they can tell is to study how often it has erupted before. ← facts
Another way they can tell is to use a special instrument called a <u>tiltmeter</u>. They use this instrument to measure whether the ground is rising. Scientists also use an instrument called a <u>gas detector</u>. It measures the amount of gas in the air.

When scientists think an eruption is coming, they warn people and tell them to ← subtopic
leave. In parts of Japan and Ecuador, ← facts
towns conduct volcano drills. These are like fire drills. Scientists have saved many lives with their research.

Friendly Letter

A person writes to someone he or she knows in a **friendly letter**. A friendly letter has five parts: a heading, a greeting, a body, a closing, and a signature. In the heading, the writer includes a comma between the name of the city and state and between the date of the month and the year.

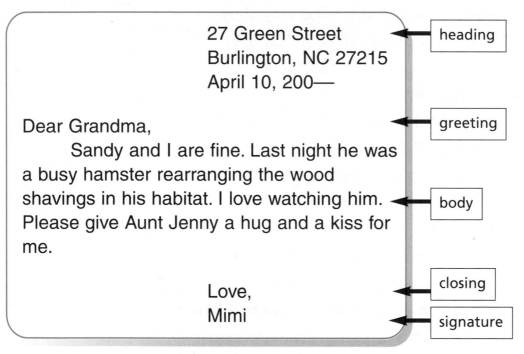

27 Green Street — heading
Burlington, NC 27215
April 10, 200—

Dear Grandma, — greeting

    Sandy and I are fine. Last night he was a busy hamster rearranging the wood shavings in his habitat. I love watching him. — body
Please give Aunt Jenny a hug and a kiss for me.

    Love, — closing
    Mimi — signature

Invitation

In an **invitation**, a writer asks someone to a party or another event. A letter of invitation has the same parts as a friendly letter. It also tells what the event is, when it will be, and where it will take place. Also, it asks for a response.

27 Green Street
Burlington, NC 27215
April 10, 200— | heading

Dear Wanda, | greeting

    Please come to a sleepover party this weekend at my house. My mom will pick you up on Friday. On Saturday we will go skating. I hope you can come. Please call by Wednesday to let me know. | body

Your friend, | closing
Mimi | signature

Thank-You Note

When someone helps you or gives you a gift, it is good manners to write a **thank-you note**.

27 Green Street
Burlington, NC 27215
April 10, 200—

Dear Sheila,

Thank you for helping me catch my hamster, Sandy, this weekend. I was afraid I had lost him forever. Your idea to put out some food and water at night was a good one. I hope you can visit again soon. I promise to leave Sandy in his habitat next time.

Your friend,
Mimi

heading

greeting

body

closing

signature

Envelope

A letter or a note is sent in an **envelope**. The envelope shows the *receiver's address* and the *return address*. The address needs a *postal abbreviation* for the state and a *ZIP code*.

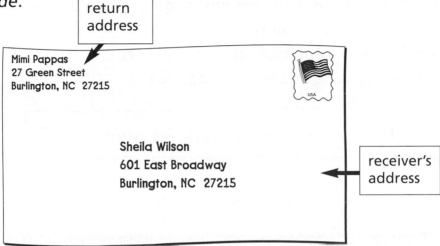

return address

Mimi Pappas
27 Green Street
Burlington, NC 27215

Sheila Wilson
601 East Broadway
Burlington, NC 27215

receiver's address

Postal Abbreviations

Alabama AL	Kentucky KY	Ohio OH
Alaska AK	Louisiana LA	Oklahoma OK
Arizona AZ	Maine ME	Oregon OR
Arkansas AR	Maryland MD	Pennsylvania PA
California CA	Massachusetts MA	Rhode Island RI
Colorado CO	Michigan MI	South Carolina SC
Connecticut CT	Minnesota MN	South Dakota SD
Delaware DE	Mississippi MS	Tennessee TN
District of	Missouri MO	Texas TX
Columbia DC	Montana MT	Utah UT
Florida FL	Nebraska NE	Vermont VT
Georgia GA	Nevada NV	Virginia VA
Hawaii HI	New Hampshire NH	Washington WA
Idaho ID	New Jersey NJ	West Virginia WV
Illinois IL	New Mexico NM	Wisconsin WI
Indiana IN	New York NY	Wyoming WY
Iowa IA	North Carolina NC	
Kansas KS	North Dakota ND	

Form

You fill in information on a **form** when you enter a contest, order from a catalog, or join a club. When you fill out a form, you should do these things.

- **Read the directions before you begin.**
- **Write neatly and clearly.**
- **Give all the information the form asks for.**
- **Write everything in the correct space.**

Valley Pet Shop Order Form

Please print using a pen.

Name ___*Pappas*_____*Mimi*_____
                 Last   First

Address _____*27 Green Street*_____
                         Number & Street

___*Burlington*_____*NC*_____*27215*___
     City   State   Zip

Telephone _____*555-2445*_____

Item	Description	Total Number
VPS18	tunnel tube brush	1
VPS12	hamster food bags	2

Grammar, Usage, and Mechanics

SENTENCES

Skill Reminder

- A **sentence** tells a complete thought. It names someone or something and tells what that person or thing is or does.
- Words in a sentence are in an order that makes sense.
- A sentence always begins with a capital letter and ends with an end mark.

Read each group of words. Write *sentence or not a sentence*.

1. **A funny story about elephants.**
2. **D.W. had a good story idea.**
3. **Arthur should tell about his puppy.**
4. **Reading books in the library.**
5. **Was the story interesting?**

Rewrite each sentence. Put the words in an order that makes sense. Begin each sentence with a capital letter and end with an end mark.

6. **a Buster notebook has.**
7. **like you Buster's did story?**
8. **enjoyed story his very much i.**
9. **about it me tell.**

SENTENCES

This story tells how Arthur and Keri made lemonade one day. Read the paragraph below. The first sentence is missing. Write a good first sentence for the story.

1. **Keri and Arthur squeezed about 100 lemons. Then they added sugar and water. Keri stirred the lemonade with a spoon and tasted it.**

Here's more of Arthur's story. Write each sentence correctly.

2. **too it sour was.**

3. **sugar added they more.**

4. **added ice they.**

5. **stirred Keri again the lemonade.**

Finish Arthur's story by adding words to each word group. Write two complete sentences to tell what happened next.

6. **Arthur tasted**

7. **Finally just right**

8. **They offered some**

CUMULATIVE REVIEW

Read each group of words. If a word group is a sentence, write *sentence.* If a word group is not a sentence, add words to make it a complete sentence. Be sure to begin each sentence with a capital letter and end with an end mark.

1. the first story

2. Arthur's sister found the story boring.

3. the second story

4. Did you find the story confusing?

5. the other children

Write each sentence, putting the words in an order that makes sense. Begin each sentence with a capital letter and end with an end mark.

6. dog i wanted always a.

7. business opened a pet arthur.

8. lot was a work of it.

9. lose Arthur did a dog?

10. the puppies one he kept of.

STATEMENTS AND QUESTIONS

Write each sentence, adding the correct end mark. Then write *statement* or *question*.

1. Do you jump rope
2. I like to jump rope
3. Here are two ropes
4. How many times did you jump
5. I won the game

Write whether each sentence is a statement or a question. Then write each sentence. Change each question to a statement. Change each statement to a question.

6. The girls are jumping rope
7. Are the twins playing
8. Can we play double Dutch
9. Tanya will turn the rope
10. Is Mandy a great jumper

STATEMENTS AND QUESTIONS

1.–3. Rosa and Marta are telling their parents what happened to Colleen's keys. Finish each sentence in the cartoon balloons by adding the correct end mark.

1. What did you do today, girls

2. I made some new friends

3. She also rescued Colleen's house key from a grate

4.–6. Add words and end marks to write complete statements or questions.

4. How did

5. I used

6. Colleen

CUMULATIVE REVIEW

Add words to make each word group a complete sentence. Write each sentence. Begin each sentence with a capital letter and end with the correct end mark.

1. kept kicking the can
2. the smell of chicken soup
3. stuck on the refrigerator
4. a baby laughing
5. pulled the string up
6. I just finished

Write each sentence, adding the correct end mark.

7. Marta's family moved
8. Rosa kept her side of the room clean
9. Did Marta bring her collections with her
10. Rosa has a new friend
11. Will Marta make some new friends
12. Her new neighbors are very nice

ARMSTRONG MOVERS

COMMANDS AND EXCLAMATIONS

- A **command** is a sentence that gives an order or a direction. End a command with a period (.).
- An **exclamation** is a sentence that shows strong feeling. End an exclamation with an exclamation point (!).

Tell whether each sentence is a command or an exclamation. Then write each sentence, adding the correct end mark.

1. **Feed that duck some crumbs**
2. **What a loud quack it has**
3. **How pretty its feathers are**
4. **Please take its picture**
5. **Wow, it's flapping its wings**

Rewrite each sentence. Begin each with a capital letter and add the correct end mark.

6. **hold this snake carefully**
7. **what a loud hiss it makes**
8. **be gentle with it**
9. **what soft skin snakes have**
10. **put it back into the weeds**

COMMANDS AND EXCLAMATIONS

Ronald is going home from camp. Find the exclamations and commands. Write each sentence, adding the correct end mark. Then tell whether the sentence is an *exclamation* or a *command*.

1. **Ronald: What a good time I had**

2. **Father: Please help me load the car**

3. **Father: Get in the car, everyone**

4. **Aunt Ruth: My, what a long trip it is**

5. **Mother: Look at the map, Ronald**

6. **Ronald: Hooray, I see our town**

Continue the scene. Write a sentence for each person. Use the kind of sentence named in parentheses ( ).

7. **Mother: (exclamation)**

8. **Father: (command)**

9. **Ronald: (exclamation)**

10. **Aunt Ruth: (command)**

CUMULATIVE REVIEW

If a word group is a sentence, write *sentence*. If a word group is not a sentence, rewrite the word group, adding words to make it a sentence.

1. **The camping trip.**
2. **I gave her some raisins.**
3. **Gave the duck a cracker.**
4. **Practiced my song.**
5. **We rolled down the hill.**

Write each sentence, adding the correct end mark. Write *statement, question, command,* or *exclamation* after each sentence.

6. **I surprised two rabbits in the field**
7. **Are there many rabbits here**
8. **Shoo them away, Dave**
9. **How floppy their ears look**
10. **Please carry my pail for me**

SUBJECTS AND PREDICATES

Write the subject of each sentence.

1. **Allie's house is near the fire station.**
2. **Mr. Puchinsky is the fire captain.**
3. **He runs the fire station.**
4. **A fire captain has an important job.**
5. **Allie's father waves to the fire captain.**
6. **The firefighters respond to an alarm.**

Write the predicate for each sentence.

7. **The little dog barks at Allie.**
8. **She gives him a biscuit.**
9. **The firefighters like Domino.**
10. **He is friendly and helpful.**
11. **The dog plays with the children at the playground.**
12. **The cat hides under a car.**

SUBJECTS AND PREDICATES

Read Allie's thank-you letter to her father. Write the subject and the predicate for each numbered sentence.

Dear Daddy,

(1) I love my new basketball. (2) You are the best father in the world. (3) My friends practiced in the park today. (4) Everybody had a good time. (5) That brand-new basketball got a real workout.

Love,

Allie

Allie wrote about her basketball dream. Help her complete each sentence. Write each sentence below, adding a subject or a predicate.

6. **Basketball**
7. **My father**
8. **watched games on television.**
9. **went to a professional game.**
10. **A good athlete**

CUMULATIVE REVIEW

Write each sentence, adding the correct end mark.

1. **Allie bounced the ball on the sidewalk**

2. **What a nice sound it makes**

3. **Can you shoot a basket**

4. **Shoot some baskets with me**

Write each sentence. Underline the subject once and the predicate twice.

5. **Allie kicked the ball.**

6. **She aimed at the basket.**

7. **Allie's new basketball hit the backboard.**

8. **Julio liked the game of basketball.**

Write one of each kind of sentence. Be sure each is a complete sentence, and use the correct end mark.

9. **Statement**

10. **Question**

11. **Command**

12. **Exclamation**

COMPOUND SUBJECTS AND PREDICATES

Skill Reminder

- A **compound subject** is two or more subjects that share a predicate.
- A **compound predicate** is two or more predicates that share a subject.
- Use commas to separate three or more subjects or predicates.

Write each sentence. Underline the compound subject. Add commas where they belong.

1. Amy and her teammates stayed at a hotel.
2. The coach and the team's doctor worked together.
3. Fans photographers and sportscasters are ready.
4. Amy her coach and the other Americans smile.

Write each sentence. Underline the compound predicate. Add commas where they belong.

5. The United States picks good athletes and trains them well.
6. Amy breathes deeply stretches and hopes for the best.
7. She won a gold medal and broke a record!
8. The people in the stands cheer stamp and sing.

COMPOUND SUBJECTS AND PREDICATES

Rewrite each group of words to make it a complete sentence. Each sentence should have a compound subject or a compound predicate.

1. **my swim goggles**
2. **the shovel**
3. **walk along the beach**
4. **swim underwater**
5. **my older brother**

Use the objects in the pictures to help you write three sentences of your own. Write at least one sentence with a compound subject and at least one sentence with a compound predicate.

CUMULATIVE REVIEW

Choose the best way to write each underlined section.

Amy Van Dyken overcame poor health and became a swimming champion. (1) One time she had to be carried off. On a stretcher (2) What a disappointment that was! (3) Amy and her coach worked out a plan. Her doctor worked out a plan, too. (4) She kept swimming. Won a bronze medal.

1. One time she had to be carried off. While on a stretcher.

   One time she had to be carried off, she was on a stretcher.

   One time she had to be carried off on a stretcher.

   No mistake

2. what a disappointment that was

   What a disappointment that was.

   what a disappointment that was?

   No mistake

3. Amy and her coach, her doctor worked out a plan.

   Amy her coach, and her doctor worked out a plan.

   Amy, her coach, and her doctor worked out a plan.

   No mistake

4. She kept swimming and won a bronze medal.

   She kept swimming she won a bronze medal.

   She kept swimming. She won a bronze medal.

   No mistake

COMPOUND SENTENCES

Write each compound sentence correctly. Use a comma and the joining word *and* or *but*.

1. Gloria gave him a kiss and he gave her a pat.

2. Officer Buckle thought of a safety tip, he was excited.

3. Gloria is fine alone but she is better with Officer Buckle.

4. Claire wrote a letter, Officer Buckle enjoyed it.

5. Officer Buckle was popular but he did not know why.

Write each sentence. Add commas where they belong.

6. The children liked the officer but they liked Gloria more.

7. The students listened to the talk and they cheered afterward.

8. Everyone enjoyed the talk and we all learned about safety.

9. Gloria wagged her tail and officer Buckle tipped his cap.

COMPOUND SENTENCES

Rewrite the letter. Use each pair of sentences to write a compound sentence. Use joining words and commas correctly. Then sign your name.

Dear Officer Buckle,

(1) I liked your talk. My friends also liked it. (2) We knew some safety rules. You taught us many new ones. (3) We remember most of your safety rules. We forgot a few.
(4) May we send you questions? Will you send us answers?
(5) Please come back. Don't forget to bring Gloria!

Sincerely,

Check your new letter. Have you used commas correctly?

CUMULATIVE REVIEW

Read each group of words. If a word group is a sentence, write *complete sentence*. If a word group is not a sentence, rewrite it to make it a complete sentence.

1. **Officer Buckle**

2. **Officer Buckle and Gloria gave their talk together.**

3. **Got bored and began to yawn.**

Read each sentence. Then tell whether it has a *compound subject* or *compound predicate.*

4. **Cal and I went to the talk.**

5. **We laughed and cheered.**

6. **Officer Buckle and Gloria were great!**

Join each pair of sentences to make a compound sentence. Write each compound sentence correctly, using the word in parentheses ( ).

7. **Gloria is just a dog. She is smarter than most dogs. (but)**

8. **Officer Buckle teaches safety. He wants children to stay safe. (and)**

COMMON AND PROPER NOUNS

- A **common noun** names any person, animal, place, or thing.

- A **proper noun** names a particular person, animal, place, or thing.

- Each important word of a proper noun begins with a capital letter.

Write each sentence. Circle the common and proper nouns.

1. **Yuko swept the sand.**

2. **The turtle came out of the Pacific Ocean.**

3. **Her eggs had leathery shells.**

4. **Taro enjoyed being with his old friend.**

5. **Jiro-San knew about the ocean.**

Copy the chart. For each common noun, write a proper noun. For each proper noun, write a common noun.

COMMON	PROPER
6. teacher	
7.	California
8. cat	
9.	Monday
10. building	

COMMON AND PROPER NOUNS

Read the story below. Then copy the chart. Complete the chart by writing each noun in the correct place. If the noun is proper, write *P* after it in the chart.

Taro lived in Japan, in a house near the Pacific Ocean. One Sunday in September, he went to visit his friend. Jiro-San used a broom to sweep the sand and make the beach safe. Later, the boy saw a turtle in Uchiura Bay. He named it Trixie.

PERSON

PLACE

ANIMAL

THING

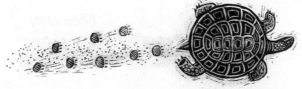

CUMULATIVE REVIEW

Read each sentence. Then tell whether it has a *compound subject* or *compound predicate,* or is a *compound sentence.*

1. The brother and his sister walked quickly.
2. The children were late, and the old man was waiting.
3. One turtle came out of the sea and laid some eggs.
4. Taro, Yuko, and Jiro-San watched.
5. The eggs hatched in September, and the beach was full of baby turtles.

Write each sentence. Circle the nouns. Write *C* above common nouns and *P* above proper nouns. Then rewrite each sentence, using capital letters to begin proper nouns.

6. The children live in japan.
7. Uchiura bay is on the pacific ocean.
8. Some children thought jiro-san was strange, but taro liked him.

SINGULAR AND PLURAL NOUNS

- A **singular noun** names one person, animal, place, or thing.
- A **plural noun** names more than one person, animal, place, or thing.
- Add *-s* or *-es* to make most nouns plural. For nouns that end in a consonant and *y,* change *y* to *i* and add *-es.*

Write each sentence. Circle the nouns. Then write *S* above each singular noun. Write *P* above each plural noun.

1. **Please put these photographs in the album.**
2. **Where is the picture of the four hawks?**
3. **Their wings are as wide as our car.**
4. **Those birds live high in the mountains.**
5. **Always take your camera on trips.**

Write the plural form of each singular noun. Write the singular form of each plural noun.

6. **eagle**
7. **holidays**
8. **hill**
9. **kisses**
10. **berry**

11. **bunnies**
12. **guppy**
13. **branches**
14. **wish**
15. **matches**

SINGULAR AND PLURAL NOUNS

Write the plural form of the noun in parentheses ( ).

1. Three (turtle) were on a beach.

2. They laid their (egg) in the wet sand.

3. Four (seagull) flew overhead.

4. Some (fly) were on one turtle.

5. There are many (beach) on this island.

Rewrite each sentence, using the plural form of the underlined noun. Each new sentence is started for you.

6. The <u>canary</u> flew into the tree.

   Two

7. A <u>spider</u> crawled on the leaf.

   A few

8. One <u>branch</u> fell during a storm.

   Three

9. One <u>flower</u> bloomed on the bush.

   Five

CUMULATIVE REVIEW

Rewrite each sentence. Write proper nouns correctly, and add the correct end mark.

1. **Aunt rita took me to a zoo**

2. **The zoo is in chicago**

3. **What an exciting trip that was**

4. **Has pablo seen the penguins**

5. **Come with us next time**

Write each sentence. Circle the nouns. Write *S* above the singular nouns. Write *P* above the plural nouns. For each singular noun, write the plural form next to the sentence.

6. **Some rabbits were near the bush.**

7. **The birds sat on their perch.**

8. **Our cousins have arrived from the city.**

9. **My parents cook our meal.**

10. **Our friends fill the day with activities.**

MORE PLURAL NOUNS

- Some nouns change their spelling in the plural form.
- Some nouns have the same spelling for both the singular and plural forms.

Draw each chart. Complete the chart of singular and plural nouns. Use a dictionary if you need to.

SINGULAR	PLURAL
1. woman	
2. mouse	
3.	geese
4. foot	
5.	teeth
6. child	
7. deer	
8. moose	
9. trout	
10.	sheep
11.	fish
12. man	

MORE PLURAL NOUNS

1.–5. Read this paragraph. Write the five nouns that have irregular plurals.

The men and women traveled toward a river. There they saw a lonely moose. Suddenly, twelve geese took off from the riverbanks. They flew a foot above the trees.

Draw the chart. Write the singular and plural forms of each noun you wrote above. Use a dictionary if you need to.

SINGULAR	PLURAL
6.	
7.	
8.	
9.	
10.	

CUMULATIVE REVIEW

Write each sentence. Circle the nouns. Write *C* above common nouns and *P* above proper nouns. Then rewrite the proper nouns correctly.

1. I got a letter on tuesday.

2. It was from alaska.

3. My uncle lived in nome.

4. bill, my cousin, sent me a picture.

5. It showed a statue of balto.

Write the correct plural form of each singular noun. Use a dictionary if you need to.

6. man

7. child

8. city

9. horse

10. tooth

11. baby

12. doctor

13. building

14. deer

15. couch

SINGULAR POSSESSIVE NOUNS

Skill Reminder

- A **possessive noun** tells who or what something belongs to.
- A **singular possessive noun** shows ownership by one person or thing. Add an apostrophe (') and an *s* to a singular noun to show ownership.

Write the possessive noun in each sentence.

1. **We saw George's eggs in the nest.**

2. **The dinosaur's name should be Georgina.**

3. **The mother's eggs will become baby dinosaurs.**

Write the possessive form of the noun in parentheses ( ).

4. **(Mr. dePaola) story is a fairy tale.**

5. **The (story) characters are cave dwellers.**

6. **The (author) story is not real.**

7. **A dinosaur could never be a (boy) pet.**

8.–10. Choose three nouns from the box. Write three sentences, using the possessive form of the nouns you chose.

woman	baby	writer	student	teacher

SINGULAR POSSESSIVE NOUNS

Follow the directions to change each singular noun.

1. **animal + apostrophe + *s* =**
2. **boy + apostrophe + *s* =**
3. **cave dweller + apostrophe + *s* =**
4. **aunt + apostrophe + *s* =**
5. **chief + apostrophe + *s* =**
6. **mother + apostrophe + *s* =**

Write a sentence for each pair of nouns. Use the possessive form of the first noun to show ownership of the second noun. An example is done for you.

Example: train tracks

The train's tracks were being fixed.

7. **caveman club**
8. **dinosaur egg**
9. **baby toy**
10. **artist picture**
11. **dog tail**
12. **student desk**

CUMULATIVE REVIEW

Read the passage and choose the word that belongs in each space.

Was George a good pet? He ate all the leaves off all the (1). The (2) cave was lit with eight (3). When George sneezed, it was a disaster.

George had four very big (4). All of (5) pots were broken. Later on, George laid some eggs. What would (6) (7) look like?

Perhaps Little Grunt should have had a (8) for a pet.

1. bush
    bushes
    bushies
    bush's

2. tribe
    tribes
    tribe's
    tribies

3. torches
    torche's
    torchs
    torch

4. foot
    feet
    foots
    feets

5. Mama
    Mamas'
    Mama's
    Mamas

6. Georges
    George's
    Georges'
    Georg's

7. baby
    babys
    babyes
    babies

8. sheep
    sheeps
    sheep's
    sheepes

PLURAL POSSESSIVE NOUNS

- A **plural possessive noun** shows ownership by more than one person or thing.
- To show ownership, add only an apostrophe (') to a plural noun that ends in *s*.

Write the possessive noun.

1. These kites' tails are made of rags.
2. People admire the kids' kites.
3. My parents' newspapers made a good kite.
4. Can you see those boys' kites up there?
5. The kites are as colorful as those birds' wings.

Write the possessive form of the plural noun in parentheses ( ).

6. The (DeWettes) house is next door.
7. The (grown-ups) car is in the driveway.
8. Their (sons) bicycles are nearby.
9. The (boys) toys are scattered.
10. Julian plays with his (friends) toys.
11.–12. Choose two plural nouns from the box below. Write two sentences. Use the plural possessive form of each noun you choose.

boys	girls	adults	playmates	robins

PLURAL POSSESSIVE NOUNS

Write the plural form of each noun. Then write the plural possessive form.

1. **playmate**
2. **schoolgirl**
3. **mother**
4. **family**
5. **brother**

6.–10. Use each plural possessive noun you wrote above in a sentence.

CUMULATIVE REVIEW

Draw each chart. Then write the correct forms of each noun.

SINGULAR	PLURAL	SINGULAR POSSESSIVE	PLURAL POSSESSIVE
1. lion			
2. thrush			
3. giraffe			
4. butterfly			
5. fox			

Write the correct possessive form of the singular or plural noun in parentheses ( ).

6. The (zoo) hours are 8:00 A.M. to 6:00 P.M.

7. Gloria admires the (monkeys) playground.

8. Where is the (bears) pen?

9. Look at the baby (gorilla) toy.

10. Julian is amazed at the (elephants) size.

ABBREVIATIONS

- An **abbreviation** is a short way to write a word. Use a period after most abbreviations.
- Begin abbreviations for proper nouns with capital letters.

Write the abbreviation that goes with each word.

1. **Monday**
2. **March**
3. **Mister**
4. **Friday**
5. **February**

Rewrite the abbreviations correctly.

6. **mr Jay**
7. **ms Grey**
8. **oct 19**
9. **mrs Pitt**
10. **Oak rd**

11. **aug 9**
12. **thurs**
13. **Loon ave**
14. **wed**
15. **dr Sanchez**

Find the words in the following sentence that could be abbreviated. Write the abbreviations.

On Tuesday, April 3, Mister Lunez is taking our class to the museum on Danby Avenue to see artworks about United States history.

ABBREVIATIONS

Help Beany organize her address book in alphabetical order. Put the last names in alphabetical order. Write the people's names, addresses, and birthdays in the correct order. Use abbreviations for titles, streets, and months.

1. **Mister George Adams**
   15 Myrtle Avenue
   September 5

2. **Doctor Rita Arnez**
   72 Pleasant Street
   October 30

3. **Mistress Gertie Boyle**
   3221 Holly Avenue
   February 20

4. **Mister John Creasey**
   624 Beach Road
   August 3

5. **Mistress Ann Coe**
   798 Pilgrim Road
   December 18

6. **Mister Myron Bates**
   320 Lombard Street
   March 1

CUMULATIVE REVIEW

Rewrite each sentence. Begin and end it correctly.

1. our playground has new swings
2. two of them are tire swings
3. each one can hold two people
4. my friend Carol Ann swings with me
5. leo pushes us higher and higher

Write each plural possessive noun and each abbreviation correctly.

6. boys gym
7. dr fry
8. sept 10
9. sky st
10. mr otis
11. dec 4
12. girls team
13. ladies room
14. thurs
15. ms Babbitt

SINGULAR AND PLURAL PRONOUNS

- A **singular pronoun** takes the place of a singular noun. Always capitalize the pronoun *I*. Singular pronouns include *I, me, you, he, she, him, her,* and *it*.

- A **plural pronoun** takes the place of a plural noun. Plural pronouns include *we, us, you, they,* and *them*.

Write the two pronouns in each sentence.

1. **I told you about the class for Visiting Dogs.**

2. **We first watched it last September.**

3. **You can join us at the next class.**

4. **He and she are teachers.**

5. **I will ask them where to meet.**

Rewrite each sentence. Use a singular or plural pronoun to replace each underlined phrase.

6. **That boy wants a visitor.**

7. **Ask those dog owners for their ideas.**

8. **Show the leash to that dog.**

9. **The dogs learned the rules right away.**

SINGULAR AND PLURAL PRONOUNS

People in the hospital enjoy receiving visitors. Read this thank-you note. The writer has repeated many nouns. Rewrite the thank-you note, using a pronoun to replace each underlined word or phrase. Underline the pronouns you used.

Dear Rosie,

Lisa would like to thank Rosie for visiting last week. Lisa really enjoyed the visit. The visit cheered Lisa up!

Sometimes the hospital is fun, but often the hospital is dull. The nurses try hard. However, the nurses have too much to do. Visitors are important. Lisa and the other patients all look forward to visitors. Please come to visit Lisa and the other patients again.

Your friend,

Lisa

CUMULATIVE REVIEW

Write the abbreviations correctly. Add capital letters if necessary.

1. dr Deeds
2. ms Sands
3. aug 4
4. jan 15
5. River rd
6. oct 31
7. mon
8. Elm st
9. mar 10
10. mrs luz

Rewrite each sentence. Use a singular or plural pronoun to replace each underlined phrase.

11. <u>The mice</u> ran around the cage.
12. <u>The mouse</u> ran around the cage.
13. The mouse looked at <u>the child</u>.
14. The mouse looked at <u>the children</u>.
15. <u>Jesse and Kelly</u> caught the mouse.

SUBJECT PRONOUNS

- A **subject pronoun** takes the place of one or more nouns in the subject of a sentence. Subject pronouns include *I, you, he, she, it, we,* and *they.*

- Always capitalize the pronoun *I.*

Write the pronoun in each sentence.

1. **She always hits home runs.**

2. **Today we will see José's talent.**

3. **He catches fly balls.**

4. **They fly far overhead.**

5. **I respect José's talent.**

Rewrite each sentence. Use a subject pronoun to replace the underlined word(s).

6. **José caught a high fly ball.**

7. **His father and I clapped wildly.**

8. **His teammates tossed their caps in the air.**

Rewrite the sentence correctly.

9. **Carmen and i practice hitting.**

SUBJECT PRONOUNS

José wrote to a friend to tell him about playing baseball. Help José finish his letter. Choose the correct subject pronouns from the box.

I	You	He	We	They

Dear Sam,

    (1) really like our new coach, Mr. Deebs. **(2)** works us very hard. **(3)** would be so tired after one of our practices!

    Carmen and her teammates are doing well. **(4)** might win the pennant. **(5)** are both lucky to have a father who loves baseball.

                Your friend,

                José

6.–10. Write five sentences, using each subject pronoun from the box.

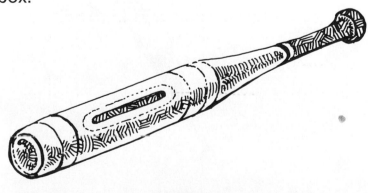

Write each sentence. Draw one line under the complete subject and two lines under the complete predicate.

1. The players practice every day.
2. Coach Lane teaches them.
3. Our team does well in the play-offs.
4. We finish third overall.
5. It pleases our parents and our coach.

Write each sentence. Use a subject pronoun to replace each underlined word or phrase. Then write *S* if the subject is singular or *P* if the subject is plural.

6. The pitchers are warming up.
7. Carmen and I take practice swings.
8. Mr. Mendez watches from the stands.
9. The pitcher's mound seems far away.
10. Carmen is the most valuable player.

OBJECT PRONOUNS

- An **object pronoun** follows an action verb or a word such as *about, at, for, from, near, of, to,* or *with.* Object pronouns include *me, you, him, her, it, us,* and *them.*

- Use *I* and *me* last with other nouns and pronouns.

Write the object pronoun in each sentence.

1. **Ramona hugs her gently.**

2. **That baby is fond of you.**

3. **Father carried the baby with him.**

4. **Mother shows us the baby gifts.**

5. **Beezus puts them upstairs.**

Rewrite each sentence. Use an object pronoun to replace each underlined phrase.

6. **Roberta dropped <u>the rattle</u>.**

7. **Ramona poured tea for <u>the dolls</u>.**

8. **Beezus tossed the ball to <u>Ramona and me</u>.**

Write these sentences correctly.

9. **Give the bottles to me and Ramona.**

10. **The baby smiled at Beezus and I.**

OBJECT PRONOUNS

Choose the correct object pronoun from the box below to replace the underlined words.

them	her	it	him	us

1. **I threw the ball to <u>the tallest boy</u>.**
2. **Beezus likes to play with <u>our baby sister</u>.**
3. **I told my class at school about <u>Beezus and the baby</u>.**
4. **They made a card for <u>my family and me</u>.**
5. **Daddy taped <u>the card</u> to the refrigerator.**

Ramona wrote about her new sister. Rewrite her sentences correctly.

I can't wait to play with she.

Will she share a room with I?

Beezus will beat me and her at games.

CUMULATIVE REVIEW

Choose the best way to write each underlined section.

(1) <u>Ramona and me are friends.</u> She has a new little sister.
The two girls share a (2) <u>room, and it gets along well.</u> The older
sister is named Beezus. (3) <u>She goes to a different school.</u>
(4) <u>Her and my sister</u> are in a club together.

1. Ramona and I are friends.
   I and Ramona are friends.
   Ramona and i are friends.
   No mistake

2. room, it gets along well.
   room gets along well.
   room, and they get along well.
   No mistake

3. It goes to a different school.
   He goes to a different school.
   A different school she goes.
   No mistake

4. My sister and her
   My sister and he
   She and my sister
   No mistake

ADJECTIVES

- An **adjective** is a word that describes a noun. An adjective can come before the noun it describes. It can follow a verb such as *is* or *seems*.

Write the adjective that describes each underlined noun.

1. The <u>desert</u> is dry.

2. Many <u>animals</u> live there.

3. A <u>cactus</u> is thorny.

4. We saw a red <u>flower</u>.

5. Little <u>water</u> reaches the plants.

6. The <u>desert</u> is also hot.

Write each adjective and the noun it describes.

7. The sly <u>coyote</u> had a bow.

8. He built a huge <u>ladder</u>.

9. The ladder reached the faraway <u>sky</u>.

10. Coyote climbed for many <u>days</u>.

11. On the cool <u>moon</u>, he rested.

12. He enjoyed the starry <u>night</u>.

ADJECTIVES

1.–10. Read the story about Coyote. Write each adjective and the noun it describes.

Coyote woke on a cold morning. He met big Bear and tiny Roadrunner near the river.

"We are going to race," said Bear. "Who will win? Make a guess."

Coyote thought for a long minute. Bear was strong. Roadrunner was fast. "I choose Roadrunner," he said.

Away they ran. Suddenly Bear stepped on a sharp stone. Then Roadrunner tripped over a spiny cactus. The runners were sad.

"Cheer up," said Coyote. "Both of you win, and you can still be best friends."

Use each adjective in the box to write a sentence about Coyote.

clever	happy	noisy	proud

CUMULATIVE REVIEW

Choose the correct pronoun in parentheses ( ).

1. (We, Us) like the view of the desert.
2. The hotel manager is speaking to (I, me).
3. (She, Her) warns us about the coyotes.
4. Please describe them to (we, us).
5. (I, Me) heard a coyote last night.

Think of an adjective to describe each underlined noun. Write each sentence, adding the adjective.

6. I admire the <u>cactus</u>.
7. What a <u>view</u> this is!
8. A <u>lizard</u> basks in the sun.
9. Our <u>car</u> is parked outside.
10. The <u>sign</u> blinks off and on.

Write each sentence. Circle each adjective and underline the noun it describes.

11. Those are bright stars.
12. This is wonderful artwork.
13. I love mashed potatoes.
14. Did you see that purple car?
15. I live in a brick house.

ADJECTIVES FOR *WHAT KIND*

- Some adjectives tell **what kind**. Adjectives can describe size, shape, or color. Adjectives can describe how something looks, sounds, feels, tastes, or smells.

Write the adjectives that tell what kind.

1. **The owl woke in the bright sun.**

2. **The owl missed her little owlet.**

3. **Now the night is long.**

4. **The sad owl will not hoot.**

Write the sentence three times. Add adjectives that answer the questions in parentheses ( ).

The owl flew away.

5. **The (what size?) owl flew away.**

6. **The (what shape?) owl flew away.**

7. **The (what color?) owl flew away.**

Write an adjective that tells what kind for each word.

8. **sight**

9. **sound**

10. **touch**

11. **taste**

12. **smell**

ADJECTIVES FOR *WHAT KIND*

Look at the pictures. Choose three adjectives from the box that correctly describe each picture. Use each adjective only once.

tiny	curved	black
spotted	slender	long
large	pointed	patterned

1.

2.

3.

4.–6. Choose one of the pictures above. Write three sentences that describe it, each using one adjective you wrote for that picture.

CUMULATIVE REVIEW

Read each sentence. Write each adjective and the noun it describes.

1. **We visited a great zoo.**
2. **I liked the funny monkeys.**
3. **A bouncy seal barked at me.**
4. **I bought a red balloon.**
5. **The huge lion scared me.**

Write the nouns in each sentence. Then rewrite each sentence, adding an adjective that describes one of the nouns.

6. **A hippo shared its pen with a bird.**
7. **Students found the path to the giraffes.**
8. **Mr. Evans showed Mary the bears.**
9. **Penguins dove into the pond for fish.**
10. **A seal splashed Juan with its tail.**
11. **Jan stopped at the café for a snack.**
12. **The elephants were eating grass in a field.**

ADJECTIVES FOR *HOW MANY*

- Some adjectives tell **how many**. Not all adjectives that tell how many give an exact number.

Write the adjective that tells how many.

1. I have a collection of eight dolls.
2. Juan gave me several pieces of candy.
3. Maria brought home a few flowers.
4. The birthday cake had twenty candles.

Write the adjective that tells how many. Then rewrite each sentence, replacing each number word with an adjective that tells how many without giving an exact number.

5. Verna sent her book to three publishers.
6. She revised the book five times.
7. The book will be seventy-five pages long.
8. Forty bookstore chains will sell it.
9. It will be translated into ten languages.

10.–12. Write three sentences about your own family. Use adjectives that tell how many.

ADJECTIVES FOR *HOW MANY*

Here is a picture about one of Verna Aardema's folktales. The sentences below describe what you see. Write the adjectives that tell how many.

1. The picture shows ten lambs in a field.
2. Several reeds fill the end of the pond.
3. You can see two ducks swimming.
4. Some hills are in the distance.
5. One wolf is watching.

Draw your own picture. Then write sentences to describe it. Use adjectives that tell how many.

CUMULATIVE REVIEW

Write the adjective in each sentence and the noun it describes.

1. **The swamp was hot.**
2. **I saw a big alligator.**
3. **A pink flamingo flew by.**
4. **It rested on one leg.**
5. **Many bugs pestered us.**

Rewrite each sentence two times. The first time, add an adjective that tells what kind. The second time, add an adjective that tells how many. An example has been done for you.

Example: I saw birds. I saw red birds. I saw eleven birds.

6. **They caught fish.**
7. **Dragonflies flew around.**
8. **Raindrops fell.**
9. **The kids ate ice cream.**
10. **The books are on the shelf.**

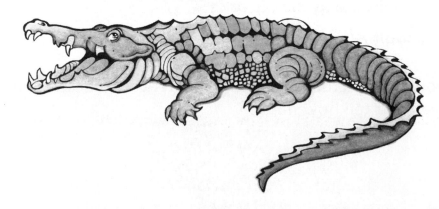

ARTICLES

- The adjectives *a, an,* and *the* are called **articles.**
- Use *a* and *an* for singular nouns. Use *the* for both singular and plural nouns. Use *a* before a word that begins with a consonant sound. Use *an* before a word that begins with a vowel sound.

Write the article in each sentence and the noun it describes.

1. **We buy food at a grocery.**
2. **In Chewandswallow, food falls from the sky.**
3. **The story is very silly.**
4. **Imagine an egg falling into your plate.**
5. **Could you eat a pizza at every meal?**

Write each sentence, using *a* or *an* to fill in the blank.

6. **Please hand me ____ fork.**
7. **I am trying to eat ____ eggplant.**
8. **It fell out of ____ cloud.**
9. **I would rather have ____ ice-cream cone.**

Write three sentences about food, using the article given.

10. **a**
11. **an**
12. **the**

ARTICLES

Here is a news story about a storm in Chewandswallow. Write the story, adding the articles *a*, *an*, or *the* where they are needed.

CHEWANDSWALLOW– (1) storm hit this small town on Wednesday night. (2) storm lasted for about (3) hour. (4) car driving down (5) main street was blown away. Luckily, (6) passengers were rescued.

   Oddly, (7) rain from this storm fell in (8) form of spaghetti and meatballs. (9) noodles wrapped themselves around buildings. They made (10) mess. (11) bulldozer was needed to remove (12) meatballs.

   (13) mayor was out of town, but twelve aldermen helped clean up. One alderman said, "This is (14) emergency. What we really need is (15) army with forks and knives!"

CUMULATIVE REVIEW

Write each sentence, adding an adjective that answers the question in parentheses ( ).

1. We visited a (what size?) farm.
2. I saw (how many?) piglets.
3. The farm had a (what color?) barn.
4. We ate some (how did they taste?) apples.
5. We fed (how many?) chickens.
6. I rode a (what color?) pony.
7. He ate (how many?) carrots.
8. The ducks made a (how did they sound?) noise.

Choose the correct article in parentheses ( ).

9. I wish I lived on (a, an) farm.
10. (An, The) animals are so wonderful!
11. Farmer Greely must be (a, an) early riser.
12. His children feed (a, the) goats.
13. The hen was sitting on (a, an) egg.
14. (An, The) pig rolled in the mud.

ADJECTIVES THAT COMPARE

- Adjectives can describe by comparing people, animals, places, or things.

- Use either *-er* or *more* with adjectives to compare two things. Use either *-est* or *most* with adjectives to compare more than two things.

Write each sentence. Circle the adjective that compares. Underline the words that tell which people or things are being compared.

1. **Molly is taller than her brother.**

2. **Meg is the quietest of the children in her family.**

3. **This house is more crowded than a stable.**

Write the correct form of the two adjectives in parentheses ( ).

4. **Was the donkey (louder, loudest) than the goat?**

5. **He was the (stronger, strongest) animal in the barn.**

6. **He was (more active, most active) than the chickens.**

Complete each sentence with the correct form of the adjective in parentheses ( ).

7. **Bartholomew was (intelligent) than anyone else.**

8. **The house seemed (calm) than it had before.**

9. **Mother was the (relaxed) of all.**

10. **The house seemed (large) without the animals.**

ADJECTIVES THAT COMPARE

Draw the chart. Complete it by writing the correct adjective that compares.

Adjective	Comparing Two Things	Comparing More Than Two Things
1. loud	louder	
2. crowded		most crowded
3. difficult		
4. small		
5. unpleasant		

6.–10. Use some of the words you wrote above to write five sentences about two crowded places.

CUMULATIVE REVIEW

Choose the best way to write each underlined section.

(1) <u>Molly is the older one of the four girls.</u> She has three sisters and four brothers. They live (2) <u>with their parents in an house</u> that is very crowded. (3) <u>It is the most frenzied household</u> you have ever seen. (4) <u>Even an animals live in the house.</u>

1. Molly is the oldest one of the four girls.

   Molly is the most old one of the four girls.

   Molly is the most oldest one of the four girls.

   No mistake

2. in an house with their parents

   with their parents in a house

   with their parents in the house

   No mistake

3. It is the frenziedest household

   It is a most frenzied household

   It is the frenzied household

   No mistake

4. Even a animals live in the house.

   Even an animal live in the house.

   Even the animals live in the house.

   No mistake

ACTION VERBS

Skill Reminder

- The **verb** is the main word in the predicate of a sentence.
- An **action verb** tells what the subject of a sentence does.

Write the action verb in each sentence.

1. The sun shone brightly.
2. No rain fell on the ground.
3. The corn died in the fields.
4. The farmers watched the sky.
5. Most of the crop failed.
6. Some families moved away.
7. Everyone hoped for better days.

Write each sentence, filling in the blank with an action verb.

8. The farmers ____ hard in their fields.
9. Grasshoppers ____ many of the leaves.
10. The wind ____ dust all around the farm.
11. The storm ____ in from the west.
12. Thunder ____ the house.

ACTION VERBS

Write each sentence, filling in the blank with an action verb.

1. Leah ____ fresh coffee cake.

2. Papa ____ the pigs and some of the cattle.

3. Mama ____ dishwater on her petunias.

4. Leah ____ her pony.

Write the action verb in each sentence.

5. **The neighbors said good-bye.**

6. **Papa borrowed money from the bank.**

7. **Leah clutched her dollar.**

8. **She bought the tractor.**

9.–10. Choose two verbs from the box. Use each verb you choose in a sentence of your own.

| dried   ruined   planted   saved |

CUMULATIVE REVIEW

Write the correct form of the adjective in parentheses ( ).

1. Leah had the (wonderful) pony of all.

2. It had a (nice) coat than any other pony.

3. Mr. B. shouted, "That's the (fine) pony in the county."

4. This year is (difficult) than last year.

Write each sentence. Begin and end each sentence correctly. Begin proper nouns with capital letters.

5. what an amazing auction we had in july

6. did the man in the big hat come from chicago

7. the family eats coffee cake every saturday

Write each sentence. Draw two lines under the predicate and circle the action verb.

8. The Great Depression began in 1929.

9. It lasted for ten years.

10. The price of farm products began to fall.

MAIN VERBS AND HELPING VERBS

Skill Reminder

- A **helping verb** works with the **main verb** to tell about an action.
- The words *have, has,* and *had* are often used as helping verbs.

Write each sentence. Underline the main verb and circle the helping verb.

1. The coyote is dreaming of a javelina dinner.
2. The javelinas could ignore the danger.
3. The coyote has chased two javelinas.
4. Their little houses have collapsed.
5. The coyote has destroyed them.

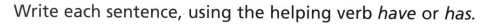

Write each sentence, using the helping verb *have* or *has.*

6. The coyote ____ called to the javelinas.
7. The clever javelinas ____ not answered.
8. Now their enemy ____ used his magic.

Use the verb shown and *have, has,* or *had* in a sentence of your own.

9. frightened
10. howled

MAIN VERBS AND HELPING VERBS

Write the story, putting the sentences in order. Underline the main verb and circle the helping verb.

    Three javelinas have moved to the desert. The javelinas have trapped him in a stove. At the third house, he has cornered all three javelinas. They have built three houses. A mean coyote has visited each house.

Write three sentences about what the javelinas might have done after they trapped the coyote. Use helping verbs and main verbs.

CUMULATIVE REVIEW

Write the main verb in each sentence.

1. Each javelina traveled a different way.

2. The coyote ran quickly and quietly.

3. What did the coyote say?

4. He will blow the tumbleweed house away.

Write each sentence, using the correct form of the helping verb *have* or *has.*

5. The woman ____ gathered saguaro ribs.

6. The two brothers ____ escaped into the desert.

7. Their sister ____ completed her house.

8. The three javelinas ____ trapped the coyote.

Write *compound subject* or *compound predicate* to describe each sentence. Then write the action verb(s).

9. A woman and a man helped the little javelinas.

10. The coyote huffed and puffed.

11. He saw the house and smelled the javelina inside.

12. The first house and the second house blew over.

PRESENT-TENSE VERBS

Skill Reminder

- A **present-tense verb** tells about action that is happening now.
- A verb must **agree** with its subject in number.
- Add *-s* or *-es* to most present-tense verbs when the subject of the sentence is *he, she, it,* or a singular noun.
- Do not add an ending when the subject is *I, you,* or a plural noun.

Write the verb. Then write an *S* if the subject is singular or a *P* if the subject is plural.

1. **The boss makes a line across the river.**
2. **Papa follows the line with the ice cutter.**
3. **They cut the ice into huge, heavy blocks.**

Write each sentence, using the correct present-tense form of the verb in parentheses ( ).

4. **The river (look) like a checkerboard.**
5. **He (watch) the snow on the ice.**
6. **I (worry) about the weather.**
7. **Papa and Uncle Jacob (step) onto the ice.**
8. **The ship (carry) ice to warm countries far away.**

9.–10. Use the verbs *freeze* and *freezes* in sentences of your own.

PRESENT-TENSE VERBS

Write each sentence, using the pronouns from the box as subjects. Use each pronoun only once. Make sure your subjects and verbs agree.

I	you	he	she	we	they

1. ____ tap holes in the ice.

2. ____ skates along the river.

3. ____ follow the ice cutter.

4. ____ stops for hot chocolate.

5. ____ shiver in the cold.

6. ____ run indoors.

7.–10. Write four sentences. For each sentence, use one present-tense verb from the box.

ride	rides	gallop	gallops

CUMULATIVE REVIEW

Write the sentences, replacing the underlined words with proper nouns.

1. The schooner comes one <u>day</u> in December.
2. <u>The man</u> walks down to the docks.
3. Will <u>your aunt</u> make hot chocolate?
4. I plan to visit <u>that state</u>.

Write the helping verb and main verb in each sentence.

5. The cacao pods have ripened.
6. Papa has opened a coconut.
7. Mama has roasted the cocoa beans.
8. She and I have crushed the beans.

Write each sentence, using the correct present-tense form of the verb in parentheses ( ).

9. The bag (smell) like pine trees.
10. The sailors (trade) ice for cocoa beans.
11. Papa (carry) me onto the ship.
12. Jacob (show) me pictures of Maine.

PAST-TENSE VERBS

Write the verb in each sentence. Then tell whether it is *present tense or past tense.*

1. **Cowboys depend on their horses.**
2. **That palomino pony jumped up.**
3. **The pony begged for apples.**

Write each sentence, using the correct past-tense form of the verb in parentheses ( ).

4. **The rider (walk) toward the black horse.**
5. **A spotted pony (graze) nearby.**
6. **The cowboy (hop) into the saddle.**
7. **The horse (whinny).**
8. **Then it (trot) around the corral.**

Use the past-tense form of each verb below in a sentence of your own.

9. **follow**
10. **skip**

PAST-TENSE VERBS

Write each sentence with the past-tense form of the underlined present-tense verb.

1. The cowboys <u>carry</u> their plates to Cookie.
2. The flapjacks <u>cook</u> quickly.
3. The cooks <u>flip</u> them over.
4. They <u>fry</u> eggs and bacon, too.
5. The eggs and bacon <u>taste</u> great.
6. After breakfast, the cooks <u>nap</u>.
7. Meanwhile, the cowboys <u>wash</u> the dishes.

Rewrite this present-tense paragraph in the past tense.

The horses sniff the air as storm clouds float overhead. Suddenly raindrops pour down. Thunderclaps scare the horses. They press against the fence.

CUMULATIVE REVIEW

Write each sentence. Use a singular or plural pronoun to replace each underlined word or phrase.

1. <u>Grandmother</u> waited for us at the ranch house.
2. <u>Dad</u> cuts wood for a new fence.
3. <u>The cowhands</u> played games every day.
4. We waved to <u>the Smithson family</u> at the rodeo.

Write each verb. Change present-tense verbs to past tense and past-tense verbs to present tense. Make sure that each present-tense verb agrees with its subject.

5. Some ranch hands chop firewood.
6. The trail boss lived on a ranch.
7. Cowhands use lariats.
8. The point riders tried a different trail.
9. The cook planned the meals.
10. Wranglers care for the horses.
11. The cowboys hurry into town.
12. One rancher purchased new clothes.

IRREGULAR VERBS

- An **irregular verb** does not end with -ed in the past tense.

Copy the chart. Write the correct form of each verb.

	VERB	PRESENT	PAST	PAST WITH HELPING VERB
1.	come	come, comes	came	
2.	do	do, does		
3.	have	have, has		
4.	say	say, says		
5.	see	see, sees	saw	

Write each sentence, using the correct past-tense form or helping verb form of the verb in parentheses ( ).

6. We (come) home from the bank.

7. We had (see) a $1,000 bill.

8. "That is a lot of money," you (say).

9.–10. Choose two irregular past-tense verbs from the chart. Use each one in a sentence of your own.

IRREGULAR VERBS

Write each sentence, using the correct form of the verb in parentheses ( ).

1. Karen (*do*—past tense with a helping verb) many chores this month.

2. She (*have*—past tense with a helping verb) to work hard.

3. Karen (*say*—past tense) she keeps her money in the bank.

4. She (*see*—past tense) the new interest rates.

5. She (*come*—past tense with a helping verb) to the bank to deposit more money.

6.–10. Rewrite this present-tense story in the past tense. Circle the past-tense verbs.

The woman comes to the bank teller's window. "I have a check for fifty dollars," she says. "Perhaps you see it on the counter. Do you?"

Read the passage and choose the word or group of words that belongs in each space.

Yesterday a store owner (1) ____ to talk to our class. I had (2) ____ her store on College Street. She (3) ____ maps and globes. She (4) ____ it was exciting to start a business. She has (5) ____ hard to make it a success. She has (6) ____ well.

1. came
   comes
   coming
   come

2. saw
   see
   seeing
   seen

3. selles
   selling
   selled
   sells

4. sayd
   say
   said
   saying

5. tryed
   tried
   tries
   trying

6. done
   did
   do
   doed

MORE IRREGULAR VERBS

Draw the chart. Complete the chart with the correct form of each verb.

VERB	PRESENT	PAST	PAST WITH HELPING VERB
1. eat	eat, eats	ate	(have, has, had)
2. give	give, gives		(have, has, had) given
3. go	go, goes		(have, has, had) gone
4. ride	ride, rides		(have, has, had) ridden
5. take	take, takes	took	(have, has, had)

Write the correct past-tense form of the verb in parentheses ( ).

6. I (eat) one apple.

7. I have (give) the others to Coyote.

8. She (take) some corn and seeds, too.

9.–10. Choose two past-tense verbs from the chart above. Use each one in a sentence.

MORE IRREGULAR VERBS

Draw the chart. Complete the chart with the correct form of each verb.

VERB	PRESENT	PAST	PAST WITH HELPING VERB
1. see	see, sees	saw	(have, has, had)
2. do	do, does	did	(have, has, had)
3. write	write, writes		(have, has, had) written
4. drive	drive, drives	drove	(have, has, had)
5. ring	ring, rings		(have, has, had) rung

Rewrite this present-tense story in the past tense.

I ride my horse into the desert. We go up a steep hill. My pony eats grass. I take a look at the moon. It gives back a shimmery light.

CUMULATIVE REVIEW

Write the past-tense form for each present-tense verb shown.

1. give
2. gleam
3. gab
4. go
5. gobble
6. see
7. slap
8. say
9. skate
10. smile

Write each sentence, using the correct helping-verb form of the verb in parentheses ( ).

11. I had (ride) in a pickup truck.
12. We have (go) to the canyon.
13. The trip has (take) four days.
14. We had never (see) a triple rainbow.
15. They have (tell) us about their trip.

THE VERB *BE*

- Forms of **the verb *be*** link the subject of the sentence to one or more words in the predicate.

- Forms of *be* tell what or where someone or something is or was.

- The subject of the sentence and the form of *be* must agree.

Write the form of *be* in each sentence and tell whether it is *present* or *past*.

1. **A roadrunner is a desert animal.**

2. **Roadrunners were everywhere.**

3. **I am very fond of roadrunners.**

4. **They are strange-looking.**

5. **A roadrunner was in my favorite cartoon.**

Write each sentence with the form of *be* asked for in parentheses ( ).

6. **You (present) in the park zoo.**

7. **He (present) with you.**

8. **We (past) on a field trip.**

9. **I (present) next to the roadrunner cage.**

10. **It (past) near some tumbleweed.**

THE VERB *BE*

Write the present-tense form of *be* that goes with each word shown.

1. I
2. **you**
3. **it**
4. **we**
5. **they**

Write the past-tense form of *be* that goes with each word shown.

6. I
7. **you**
8. **it**
9. **we**
10. **they**

Rewrite this past-tense story in the present tense.

   Alejandro was content. The animals were happy at their water hole. They were glad Alejandro was their friend. I was glad, too.

CUMULATIVE REVIEW

Draw the chart. Write the missing form of each verb.

PRESENT	PAST
1. they have	they
2. she	she was
3. it says	it
4. we go	we
5. they	they were
6. I am	I
7. he does	he

Write each sentence, changing the present-tense verbs to past tense and the past-tense verbs to present tense.

8. Visitors were welcome at Alejandro's house.

9. It is a small adobe house.

10. Alejandro had a beautiful garden.

11. We ride by in a pickup truck.

12. I was happy in the desert.

13. Some desert animals ate plants.

14. You see many kinds of plants there.

CONTRACTIONS

Write the two words that make up each contraction.

1. **Aren't mountains interesting?**

2. **You're looking at Mount Everest.**

3. **Surprisingly, it's still growing.**

4. **Don't mountains ever stop growing?**

5. **No, they aren't as still as they seem.**

Write the contraction for each pair of words.

6. **he is**   8. **I am**

7. **they are**   9. **we are**

Write each sentence, using a contraction in place of the underlined phrase.

10. **Most people <u>can not</u> climb tall mountains.**

11. **Mount Everest <u>has not</u> proved easy to climb.**

12. **I <u>would not</u> dare try it.**

CONTRACTIONS

Find the "sums." Write the contractions.

1. could + not =
2. had + not =
3. they + are =
4. I + am =
5. have + not =
6. are + not =
7. she + is =
8. we + are =
9. is + not =
10. did + not =

11.–15. Rewrite this paragraph. Replace each contraction with the two words used to form it.

The wind **isn't** kind to rocks. Slowly, **it's** wearing them down. **They're** taking on new shapes. **Don't** be alarmed. **You're** seeing nature in action.

CUMULATIVE REVIEW

Write the two words that make up each contraction. Then circle the subject pronouns and underline the forms of *be* in your answers.

1. We're going to study earthquakes.
2. Let me know when you're ready.
3. It's a long way to the library.
4. Dad says he's going to drive us.
5. I'm looking forward to learning more.

Write each sentence, replacing the underlined words with contractions.

6. I am doing a report about the Himalayas.
7. They are discussed in that book about mountains.
8. You will learn a lot from my report.
9. I would not want to climb Mount Everest.
10. It is very dangerous.

ADVERBS

- An **adverb** is a word that modifies a verb.
- An adverb may tell *where, when,* or *how* an action happens.

Write the adverb that modifies each underlined verb.

1. The armadillo often <u>sends</u> postcards.
2. He <u>walks</u> quickly to his desk.
3. The little animal <u>writes</u> beautifully.
4. He <u>mailed</u> one postcard today.
5. The postal carrier <u>came</u> early.

Tell whether the underlined adverb tells *where, when,* or *how.*

6. The armadillo sits <u>thoughtfully</u>.
7. He <u>then</u> begins a letter.
8. He <u>carefully</u> chooses some paper.
9. He writes his address <u>there</u>.
10. <u>Finally</u>, he finishes his work.

From Your Friend

Rewrite each sentence, using an adverb that gives the information in parentheses ( ).

11. I received a letter. (when)
12. The postal carrier delivered it. (where)

ADVERBS

1.–5. Read Brillo Armadillo's postcard. Write the adverbs and the verbs they describe.

> Dear Sasparillo,
>
> You write beautifully. Your stories interest me greatly. Next, tell me about Texas. You clearly love it. Visit me sometime.
>
> Your friend,
>
> Brillo

6.–10. Rewrite Sasparillo's postcard to make it more interesting. Add an adverb to describe each underlined verb.

Dear Brillo,

I <u>love</u> Texas. The mountains <u>tower</u>. The desert <u>blooms</u>. Eagles <u>fly</u>. <u>Write</u> to me!

Your friend,

Sasparillo

CUMULATIVE REVIEW

Write each sentence, replacing each contraction with the two words used to make it.

1. We're going to Texas.

2. That isn't a very big armadillo.

3. I think he's very cute.

4. Armadillos don't really write postcards.

5. It's fun to pretend, though.

6. You haven't read this book?

Write the verb and adverb in each sentence. Then tell whether the adverb describes *where, when,* or *how.*

7. The landscape changes dramatically.

8. Armadillo looked around.

9. The eagle flew upward.

10. Then the rocket ship took them.

11. The rocket flies quickly!

12. The rocket ship flew above them.

COMPARING WITH ADVERBS

- Adverbs can be used to compare two or more actions.
- Use either *-er* or *more* with adverbs to compare two actions.
- Use either *-est* or *most* with adverbs to compare more than two actions.

Write the adverb that compares. Include *more* or *most* if it is used with the adverb.

1. The Oort cloud moves more evenly than a swarm of bees.

2. One comet shot into space faster than an arrow.

3. That one broke loose most violently of all.

Write each sentence, using the correct adverb in parentheses ( ).

4. Do comets burn (hotter, hottest) than the Sun?

5. They move (more speedily, most speedily) than rocket ships.

6. They are pulled (more powerfully, most powerfully) of all.

Write the sentence, using *more* and *most* with the adverb in parentheses ( ).

7. The asteroid flew (slowly) than the comet.

8. Since the Sun is the closest star, it pulls (forcefully) on the Earth.

COMPARING WITH ADVERBS

Draw the chart. Complete the chart with the correct form of the adverb that compares.

ADVERB	COMPARING TWO ACTIONS	COMPARING MORE THAN TWO ACTIONS
1. powerfully	more powerfully	
2. loudly		most loudly
3. high		
4. cleverly		
5. quickly		

6.–10. Use some of the words you wrote above to write five sentences about the actions of aliens from other planets. Make a comparison in each sentence.

CUMULATIVE REVIEW

Read each passage, and choose the word or group of words that belongs in each space.

The comet glows (1) than a star. It (2) past the Earth. It has (3) a long time to get here. Of all the comets, that one moves (4).

Comets fly (5) through space. Someone (6) the comet's tail streaking across the sky. Astronomers long ago (7) about comets. The (8) astronomers knew comets were not stars.

1. bright
   brighter
   brightest
   most bright

2. go
   going
   goes
   go's

3. taken
   takes
   take
   taking

4. more faster
   most fastest
   faster
   fastest

5. quickly
   quicker
   quick
   most quick

6. saw
   seen
   seeing
   see

7. tell
   tells
   telling
   told

8. more smart
   most smarter
   smartest
   more smarter

Additional Practice

ADDITIONAL PRACTICE

Sentences

A. Read each group of words. Write whether each group of words is a sentence.

Examples:

Spiders are fun to watch.
sentence

Big and hairy with eight legs.
not a sentence

1. Mrs. Bentley has a special hobby.

2. She raises spiders.

3. Tarantulas are relatives of the spiders in your garden.

4. Are quiet pets!

5. Mrs. Bentley takes good care of her collection.

6. Some people think they are scary creatures!

7. Can live for thirty years.

8. One tarantula sheds its skin.

9. Crawls on her arm.

10. It does not bite her.

B. Identify each sentence. Revise each of the other groups of words so it becomes a sentence.

Example:

Peppers in Victor's garden.
Victor grows peppers in his garden.

11. Victor's mother makes delicious salsa.

12. Hot peppers, tomatoes, and onions.

13. Victor planted pepper seeds in January.

14. In milk cartons filled with soil.

15. He watered the seeds each day.

16. Saw sprouts in the carton.

17. Inside his house for weeks.

18. He planted little plants outside.

19. Pepper plants like warm weather.

20. Protected the plants from snails.

21. Victor watered the plants every day.

22. Ripe red peppers!

23. He washed them and chopped them up.

24. Delicious in tacos and on nachos!

25. Winner of the blue ribbon at the fair!

ADDITIONAL PRACTICE
Statements and Questions

A. Read the sentences. Identify each statement.

Example:

Lester travels with his parents.
statement

1. He has lived in eight countries.

2. Do you know where Rwanda is?

3. Isn't that country in Africa?

4. Lester's family lived there for years.

5. The family lived in Japan last year.

B. Read the sentences. Identify each question.

Example:

Do you know anyone who has lived in a different country?
question

6. Where does Lester live now?

7. He and his family moved to Canada.

8. Isn't Vancouver a beautiful city?

9. Does Lester study Japanese in school?

10. He studies the Japanese system of writing called *kanji*.

C. Read each sentence. Write whether it is a statement or a question. Revise each question to make it a statement.

Example:

Wasn't Elizabeth Cochrane a famous writer?

question—Elizabeth Cochrane was a famous writer.

11. She was a brave newspaper reporter.

12. Was she born in 1867?

13. Didn't she use the name Nellie Bly?

14. Were women treated poorly in jails then?

15. Cochrane went to jail to find out.

16. Did she write about what happened?

17. Were people shocked by her articles?

18. After that, the jails treated women better.

19. Was Cochrane famous by the time she was twenty-one?

20. Did she decide to travel around the world?

21. Jules Verne wrote a book about world travel.

22. Cochrane wanted to circle the globe, too.

23. Had airplanes already been invented?

ADDITIONAL PRACTICE
Exclamations and Commands

A. Read the sentences. Write which ones are exclamations.

Example:

What a special flower the dandelion is!
exclamation

   1. **This is a tasty salad!**

   2. **What are these green leaves called?**

   3. **What a surprise this is!**

   4. **I've never eaten dandelion leaves before!**

   5. **The young leaves are not bitter at all.**

B. Read the sentences. Write which ones are commands.

Example:

Dig up the roots of those dandelions.
command

   6. **Give them to Grandma.**

   7. **She will wash them and roast them.**

   8. **Please grind up the roots.**

   9. **Stay away from this boiling pot.**

  10. **Give your mother this cup of tea.**

C. Read each sentence. Write whether it is an exclamation or a command.

Example:

This town smells funny!
exclamation

11. **Try a bit of my spaghetti.**

12. **How tasty it is!**

13. **I used a whole garlic in the pot of sauce!**

14. **Leave enough in the pot for my sister.**

15. **Find Gilroy on this map of California.**

16. **You've located the garlic capital!**

17. **Come with me to the Garlic Festival.**

18. **There must be ten thousand garlic plants!**

19. **Every food at this festival has garlic!**

20. **That stand is selling garlic ice cream!**

21. **I can't believe you're really eating it!**

22. **Give me a little taste.**

23. **Take the rest of the ice cream home.**

24. **What fun we've had at the festival!**

25. **Brush your teeth for a long time tonight.**

ADDITIONAL PRACTICE

Parts of a Sentence: Subject

A. Read each sentence. Write the subject.

Example:

My brother loves apples.
my brother

1. These apples have a lovely yellow color.

2. The smell reminds him of honey.

3. Theo takes one to school every day.

4. His grandfather made an apple pie.

5. The whole family enjoyed that treat.

6. Elena prefers Northern Spy apples.

7. A large red apple sits on the sill.

8. The first bite will be the best.

9. The Green Nursery sells twenty-six kinds.

10. Each kind produces a different flavor.

Writing Application Use an encyclopedia to find information about a type of fruit. Write sentences that tell where it is grown and how people use it. Underline the subjects of your sentences.

B. Revise each group of words by adding a subject.

Example:

_____ has the most beautiful garden.
Mrs. Gonzales has the most beautiful garden.

11. _____ has a tall tree in her yard.

12. _____ are the most delicious fruit.

13. _____ are the worst pests.

14. _____ build nests in tall trees.

15. _____ bloom early in the spring.

16. _____ is my favorite flavor of jelly.

17. _____ climb trees very fast.

18. _____ need water and sunshine.

19. _____ turn red in the fall.

20. _____ flies from flower to flower.

21. _____ have very sharp thorns.

22. _____ grows quickly.

23. _____ likes strawberries.

24. _____ chases cats all the time.

25. _____ is the best place for a picnic.

ADDITIONAL PRACTICE

Parts of a Sentence: Predicate

A. Read the sentences. Write the predicate of each one.

Example:

The grocer filled a huge jar with peanuts.
filled a huge jar with peanuts

1. The local newspaper announced a contest.

2. Porter's Bicycle Shop sponsors the contest.

3. The store displays a jar in its window.

4. Each student guesses the number of peanuts in the jar.

5. Mina wants to win the grand prize very much.

6. Her brother needs a new bicycle.

7. This smart young woman estimates the size of the jar.

8. She measures some peanuts.

9. The jar can hold about 1,750 peanuts.

10. Mina's answer is closest to the correct number!

B. Write each sentence, and underline the predicate.

Example:

My aunt collects string.
My aunt <u>collects string</u>.

11. She rolls her string into a ball.

12. My aunt ties a new piece of string to the last one on the ball.

13. Each piece makes the ball a little bigger.

14. My aunt's hobby is important to her.

15. People drop pieces of string in odd places.

16. She gathers string from many places.

17. A string ball grows slowly.

18. Francis A. Johnson started a ball of string in 1950.

19. He added to it for 28 years.

20. The ball was almost 13 feet tall by 1978.

21. This amazing ball was 40 feet around.

22. Mr. Johnson became the most famous string collector in the world.

23. The ball of string became famous, too.

24. It was the largest ball of string in history.

25. A hobby can make a person famous.

ADDITIONAL PRACTICE

Nouns

A. Read each sentence. Write the nouns.

Example:

My cousin is a pilot.
cousin, pilot

1. **My best friend is a flier, too.**

2. **My pal flew over our house.**

3. **This amazing girl may fly to the moon one day!**

4. **The father is also a pilot.**

5. **This man owns a small plane.**

6. **The inside has only four seats.**

7. **The family decided to take a trip.**

8. **The aircraft had to stop for fuel.**

9. **The group reached an airport 3,000 miles away.**

10. **The passengers arrived safely.**

Writing Application Think about a trip you have taken. Write sentences to tell about the people, places, and things you saw.

B. Write the sentences. Underline the nouns.

Example:

The lake at our camp has an area where people can swim.

The <u>lake</u> at our <u>camp</u> has an <u>area</u> where <u>people</u> can swim.

11. The water is cold.

12. The boy stands on the dock.

13. A lifeguard stands nearby.

14. The child dives into the lake.

15. This young camper swims for ten minutes.

16. The counselor later shakes the hand of the swimmer.

17. This test was difficult.

18. Now this student can learn to use a canoe.

19. A paddle lies on the shore.

20. The team practices away from the rocks.

21. The man ties the boat to the dock with rope.

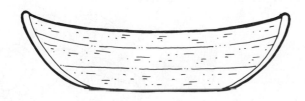

ADDITIONAL PRACTICE
Common Nouns

A. Read the sentences. Write the common nouns.

Example:

Levi Hutchins was a clockmaker.
clockmaker

1. This young person lived in Concord, New Hampshire.

2. Hutchins always started work early.

3. This fellow was awake before the sun came up.

4. Some people don't like to get up when the sky is dark.

5. Sometimes Hutchins was so tired he stayed in bed.

6. The man had an idea for a new kind of clock.

7. This machine would have a bell in it.

8. The owner would set the piece for a certain time.

9. A chime would ring then.

10. What invention did Hutchins create?

Writing Application Think about an invention you use every day. Search the Internet for information about the invention. List the information you find under the headings *people*, *places*, and *things*. Then write a paragraph about the invention.

B. Revise each sentence. Replace the underlined common nouns with other common nouns. Your sentences may be silly.

Example:

The <u>platypus</u> is an unusual <u>animal</u>.
The kangaroo is an unusual creature.

11. The <u>platypus</u> lives in Australia and Tasmania.

12. It has thick <u>fur</u> on its <u>body</u>.

13. Its <u>beak</u> is like the <u>bill</u> of a <u>duck</u>.

14. Its <u>tail</u> is like that of a <u>beaver</u>.

15. <u>Platypuses</u> live in <u>rivers</u> and <u>lakes</u>.

16. They eat <u>worms</u>, <u>snails</u>, and <u>fish</u>.

17. <u>Platypuses</u> have <u>flippers</u> instead of <u>paws</u>.

18. These furry <u>animals</u> are good <u>swimmers</u>.

19. The <u>animal</u> has sharp <u>spurs</u> on its <u>ankles</u>.

20. It will strike at an <u>enemy</u> with these <u>spurs</u>.

ADDITIONAL PRACTICE
Proper Nouns

A. The nouns in these sentences are underlined. Write each proper noun.

Example:

Pompeii was an ancient city.
Pompeii

1. A terrible thing happened in Pompeii long ago.

2. The tragedy happened in August.

3. One afternoon, the people of Italy heard an explosion.

4. A volcano named Mount Vesuvius erupted!

5. A few citizens fled toward the Mediterranean Sea.

6. Red-hot lava flowed toward the city near Naples.

7. The town of Herculaneum was also in danger that day.

8. The Metropolitan Museum shows objects the residents used there.

9. Families in some parts of Europe still worry about volcanoes.

10. Mount Etna is also a mountain there.

B. Write the proper nouns in these sentences.

Example:

Many unusual animals are in the London Zoo.
London Zoo

11. London is the capital of England.

12. Its zoo is one of the largest in Europe.

13. In 1865 an elephant from Africa was brought to the zoo.

14. The elephant, named Jumbo, was sold to a man who owned a circus.

15. His name was P. T. Barnum.

16. Queen Victoria wanted the elephant to stay in the London Zoo.

17. Barnum brought the elephant to North America anyway.

18. People in New York, Chicago, and Philadelphia went to see this huge beast.

19. Americans began saying that anything large was "jumbo-sized."

20. Some large elephants have been found in Namibia recently.

ADDITIONAL PRACTICE
Singular and Plural Nouns

A. Write the singular noun or nouns in each sentence.

Example:

Laura sends her friend postcards.
Laura, friend

1. Sarah writes letters to her pal.

2. Her sister moved to a land across the sea.

3. She needs a coat and mittens there in the winter.

4. Laura lives with her parents near the beach.

5. On many days in January she wears shorts.

B. Write the plural noun or nouns in each sentence.

Example:

Florida has many miles of beaches.
miles, beaches

6. The two friends make bracelets.

7. These treasures are kept in painted boxes.

8. Sarah sends her favorite books to her friend.

9. Laura sends drawings of a costume.

10. Sarah laughs when she sees the shoes for this costume.

C. Look at the nouns in these sentences. If the underlined noun is singular, write its plural form. If it is plural, write its singular form.

Example:

The <u>fox</u> was in the <u>shadows</u>.
foxes, shadow

11. She had a red <u>coat</u> and bright <u>eyes</u>.

12. The <u>fox</u> was watching the <u>hens</u>.

13. Sturdy <u>wire</u> and strong <u>boards</u> would keep the <u>chickens</u> safe.

14. She needed to feed her <u>kits</u>.

15. She did not see the <u>girl</u> who was watching her.

16. That <u>person</u> wanted the <u>animal</u> to be her pet.

17. A <u>horn</u> on a <u>car</u> beeped loudly.

18. The small <u>hunter</u> pricked up her <u>ears</u>.

19. An <u>airplane</u> roared overhead.

20. The little <u>creature</u> heard the <u>noises</u>.

21. She dashed off into the <u>bushes</u>.

ADDITIONAL PRACTICE

Plural Nouns Ending in *ies*

A. Proofread each sentence. Write the correct plural form of the nouns whose singular form ends in *y*.

Example:

Fernando and Haruo are buddy.
buddies

1. They have very different hobby.

2. Fernando collects penny, and Haruo trains puppy.

3. Fernando has lived in three city in Michigan.

4. Haruo has lived in three country in South America.

5. Fernando is friendly and dislikes bully.

6. Haruo likes to hear Fernando's many story.

7. Fernando loves birthday party.

8. Haruo watches plays and comedy on TV.

9. Fernando helps his mother bake many pastry.

10. Haruo helps his father make different jelly and jams.

Writing Application Make a list of foods you enjoy. Then write a few sentences about them. Be sure to use the correct form of plural nouns.

B. Revise the underlined nouns in each sentence. Write the singular form of any underlined plural noun. Write the plural form of any underlined singular noun.

Example:

Some <u>families</u> take vacations in the <u>country</u>.
family, countries

11. Dalton visits his grandmother in the <u>city</u> every summer.

12. Today the <u>sky</u> is clear and bright.

13. Dalton waters the <u>daisies</u> in the garden.

14. His grandmother cuts <u>lilies</u> for a bouquet.

15. Dalton meets old and new <u>buddies</u> at the park.

16. George invited Dalton to his birthday <u>party</u>.

17. Dalton has no <u>worries</u>.

18. He writes to his <u>family</u> every week.

19. There is a new <u>puppy</u> at his home.

20. His room has a fish tank full of <u>guppies</u>.

21. Dalton's grandmother works at the <u>library</u>.

22. Dalton likes to read <u>stories</u> about animals.

23. He also likes to read <u>mysteries</u>.

ADDITIONAL PRACTICE
Irregular Plural Nouns

A. Read each sentence. Write the noun in parentheses ( ) that fits better.

Example:

Keisha has lost her two front (tooth, teeth).
teeth

1. Keisha has gone to Dr. Chun since she was a small (child, children).

2. The (man, men) who lives next door goes to Dr. Chun, too.

3. Dr. Chun is a fine dentist and a friendly (woman, women).

4. She has toys including a mechanical (goose, geese) in her office.

5. Two of the toys are dancing (mouse, mice).

6. A big stuffed (ox, oxen) sits in a chair.

7. A cartoon about a little country (mouse, mice) hangs on the wall.

8. A pair of plastic (goose, geese) stand in the corner.

9. Many (child, children) like Dr. Chun.

10. She keeps her patients happy and their (tooth, teeth) healthy.

B. Look at the underlined noun in each sentence. Write the plural form of any underlined singular noun. Write the singular form of any underlined plural noun.

Examples:

Every <u>child</u> likes this kind of amusement park.
children

The <u>mice</u> there talk and sing.
mouse

11. **A <u>goose</u> lays golden eggs near a tree with golden leaves.**

12. **A wolf brags about his sharp <u>teeth</u>.**

13. **A giant <u>man</u> waves.**

14. **His <u>feet</u> are as large as boats.**

15. **Beside him stands a friendly blue <u>ox</u>.**

16. **One <u>woman</u> lives in an old shoe.**

17. **Many <u>children</u> crowd around her.**

18. **An angry woman chases three <u>mice</u>.**

Writing Application Write a summary of a folktale you know well. Use the correct form of plural nouns in your summary.

ADDITIONAL PRACTICE
Possessive Nouns

A. Read the sentences. Write the possessive nouns.

Example:

Chester wanted to be the first to use the class's new computer.
class's

1. The room's new computer arrived today.

2. Elena plugged in the machine's keyboard.

3. The students' eyes opened wide.

4. The monitor's screen lit up.

5. It was the school's first color monitor!

6. Ms. Aboud asked for Chester's help.

7. Chester saw Joni's sad face.

8. He wondered what his friend's problem was.

9. "I don't understand the user's handbook," whispered Joni.

10. "Soon you'll be the class's computer expert!" said Chester.

Writing Application Write a paragraph about a person who has a special skill. Use possessive nouns in your paragraph.

B. Write each sentence. Underline the possessive noun.

Example:

Vivian's class visited the seashore.
Vivian's class visited the seashore.

11. That ocean's size surprised her.

12. The sun's light was bright.

13. Vivian took Juni's picture.

14. Then Juni took Vivian's picture.

15. The group's task was to observe tide pools.

16. "This one's waves are filling it up," Juni said.

17. The two girls' tide pool was busy.

18. A crab interrupted a water bug's stroll.

19. The bug ran away from the crab's snapping claws.

20. Vivian counted a starfish's arms.

21. Juni borrowed a friend's pencil.

22. She sketched a creature's shape.

23. Vivian wanted to touch a sea urchin's spines.

24. She remembered her teacher's instructions, though.

25. "Do not disturb this pool's residents!"

ADDITIONAL PRACTICE
Singular Possessive Nouns

A. Write each possessive noun that is singular. Be careful. Not all of the sentences have a singular possessive noun.

Example

Todd's friend Daniel was playing for the Bluebirds.
Todd's

1. Daniel came up from the team's dugout.

2. He heard his teammates' cheers.

3. The pitcher tugged on his cap's bill.

4. Daniel remembered his coaches' instructions.

5. He swung at the pitcher's first pitch.

6. Daniel hit a ground ball to the shortstop's left.

7. The player's throw was too high.

8. It went over the first baseman's head.

9. Daniel's legs carried him safely to second base.

10. Later, Daniel scored the Bluebirds' first run.

B. Read these sentences. Revise the underlined words so that one of the words is a singular possessive noun.

Example:

The paws of Scooter were covered with pizza sauce.

Scooter's paws

11. The naughty dog had eaten the <u>dinner of the family</u>.

12. <u>The mother of Dina</u> was upset.

13. <u>The engine of her car</u> was not working.

14. The <u>store in town</u> had already closed.

15. Dina said she would solve that <u>problem of the day</u>.

16. She fastened <u>the strap of her helmet</u>.

17. She rode her bike to the <u>shop in the next town</u>.

18. <u>The stomach of her mother</u> was rumbling.

19. As she passed <u>the parking lot of her school</u>, she saw something in the road.

20. It was the <u>backpack of a student</u>.

21. Dina looked at the <u>cover of the backpack</u>.

22. The <u>name of the owner</u> was written on it.

23. Dina had found <u>the backpack of her best friend</u>!

ADDITIONAL PRACTICE
Plural Possessive Nouns

A. Read the sentences. Write the plural possessive nouns. Be careful. Not all sentences have a plural possessive noun.

Example:

Mr. Kozlov is the squirrels' best friend.
squirrels'

1. He sits beneath the trees' branches.

2. He pays no attention to the wind's cold, sharp air.

3. He watches the animals' quick movements.

4. Then he cracks the nuts' shells, one at a time.

5. He tosses the nuts near the oaks' roots.

6. He puts the empty shells into the park's trash can.

7. The nuts quickly disappear into the squirrels' mouths.

8. Finally, Mr. Kozlov's pockets are empty.

9. He leaves his friends' home.

10. The city's streetlights help him find his way.

B. Revise these sentences. Rewrite the underlined words so that one of the words is a plural possessive noun.

Example:

The <u>smell of hamburgers</u> made everyone hungry.

hamburgers' smell

11. Sami swept <u>the sidewalks of his neighbors</u>.

12. He heard <u>the laughter of his sisters</u>.

13. He saw <u>the kites of two boys</u>.

14. Mrs. Gomez lit <u>the barbecues of the cooks</u>.

15. She made <u>the crispy shells of the tacos</u>.

16. <u>The residents of the apartments</u> came to the party.

17. <u>The pets of the parents</u> were not invited.

18. <u>The behavior of the pets</u> had not been good last year.

19. <u>The cones of the workers</u> blocked off the street.

20. <u>The engines of the cars</u> were all silent.

21. <u>The radios of the teenagers</u> were all tuned to the same station.

22. <u>The feet of the dancers</u> moved quickly.

ADDITIONAL PRACTICE
Pronouns

A. Write the pronouns in these sentences.

Example:

Edwin called me Friday morning.
me

1. "We want you to come with us to the lake!" he exclaimed.

2. "Do you have room for me in the car?" I asked.

3. "Yes, we are borrowing Aunt Lydia's van," he answered.

4. "Are you bringing a fishing pole?" I asked.

5. "Yes, Mom and I are going to rent a rowboat for fishing," Edwin replied.

6. Then he said, "When we went to the lake in May, she caught a huge bass."

7. "Would you ask her to give me a fishing lesson?" I asked.

8. "She will be glad to teach you," Edwin said.

9. "I would love to go with you tomorrow," I said finally.

10. "Great!" said Edwin. "We will pick you up at 4 A.M."

B. Read each pair of sentences. Write a pronoun that makes sense in the blank.

Example:

This bridge is being painted. ____ must not get rusty.

It

11. Susan is a painter. ____ paints bridges.

12. The paint keeps the bridge looking clean. ____ also keeps rust from forming.

13. Brett checks the bridge. ____ looks for trouble spots.

14. Rust forms all the time. ____ forms where water settles on steel.

15. Susan climbs a ladder. ____ climbs slowly.

16. She paints an old bolt. ____ is very rusty.

17. Brett looks at the bridge cables. ____ help support the bridge.

18. You and I watch the workers. ____ think they are brave.

19. Drivers see the work truck. ____ slow down.

20. Now they are painting a bridge tower. ____ is many feet high!

ADDITIONAL PRACTICE
Singular Pronouns

A. Read the sentences. Write the singular pronouns.

Example:

I went with Natalie and Matt to the school carnival.

I

1. Natalie and I were at a picnic table.

2. She was telling me a joke.

3. Suddenly I heard a whistle blow.

4. "The three-legged race is starting!" Natalie yelled to me.

5. She and I ran to the playing field at top speed.

6. Matt waved wildly to me.

7. "Will you hop with me?" he asked.

8. Natalie looked at me, and I looked at her.

9. "I am Natalie's partner," I told him.

10. Matt raced with Robert, but Natalie and I won by a foot.

Writing Application Think about a character in a story you have read. Write a paragraph to describe the character. Be sure to use singular pronouns correctly.

B. Read each pair of sentences. Write the singular pronoun that fits with the meaning of the second sentence.

Example:

The subway train rumbled toward the station. ____ stopped at the platform.

It

11. Ned was going to a soccer match. ____ wore a jacket.

12. Ned had been waiting for twenty minutes. ____ had written a letter to pass the time.

13. Ned's mom had been reading. She had brought a newspaper with ____.

14. Ned got on the train. Ned's mom followed ____.

15. Ned stood in the crowded train car. ____ held on to a pole.

16. Ned's mom studied a map. ____ told Ned they would get off at the next stop.

17. A moment later the train slowed down. ____ was not at any station.

18. Then the train began moving faster. ____ pulled into the station.

19. Ned wanted to run ahead. ____ stayed close to his mom, though.

ADDITIONAL PRACTICE
Plural Pronouns

A. Write the plural pronouns in these sentences.

Example:

"I am glad the teacher put us in charge of art supplies," Shirley said to Omar.

us

1. "We will go to the pond today and paint," Shirley said.

2. "Won't the other class join us?" asked Omar.

3. "No, they will paint at the park today," Shirley said.

4. "Should we count the easels?" Omar asked.

5. "No, I am sure they are all here," Shirley answered.

6. "I am going to count them anyway," said Omar.

7. The two of them walked to the supply closet.

8. They found that two easels had been borrowed by the other class.

9. "We were smart to check," said Shirley.

10. "Those missing easels could have caused problems for us," she told Omar.

B. Read each pair of sentences. Write a plural pronoun that makes sense in each blank.

Example:

Lorena pointed at the clouds. "____ look dangerous!" she said.
They

11. "It looks like rain. ____ should all run to the bus," Lorena said.

12. Kim said, "Our teachers asked us to find all the plants on the list. ____ will be unhappy if we don't."

13. "Storms can be dangerous," Lorena said. "I want ____ to be safe."

14. Heavy rain began to fall on the girls. ____ ran toward the bus.

15. "I see blackberry bushes and a sugar pine tree!" said Kim. "____ are both on our list!"

16. "This is no time to stop!" said Lorena. "____ will get very wet."

17. The girls reached the school bus. "____ were worried about you!" their teachers said.

18. Kim told the teachers she had not found all the plants on the list. ____ told her not to worry.

ADDITIONAL PRACTICE
Subject Pronouns

A. Write the subject pronouns in these sentences.

Example:

I rehearsed outside with Jan last Wednesday.

I

1. We practiced all ten of our concert pieces.

2. She set down her bow and went to get some water.

3. I saw a parrot fly into the bandstand.

4. It picked up Jan's sheet music and began to fly away.

5. I yelled, "Hey, bird, put Jan's music down!"

6. I think my yelling surprised the parrot.

7. It dropped the paper.

8. We put Jan's music back on her stand.

9. She laughed at the story of the music-loving parrot.

10. Will we see the parrot on the day of our concert?

Writing Application Make up a short story in which you are the main character. As you write the story, use subject pronouns to tell about what you do, think, see, and hear.

B. Revise each sentence. Replace the underlined word or words with a subject pronoun.

Example:

<u>Anton</u> puts on his air tank.
He puts on his air tank.

11. <u>The Red Sea</u> is warm and salty.

12. <u>Many unusual fish</u> live there.

13. <u>Anton</u> will take pictures under the water.

14. <u>His sister Pam</u> will develop them.

15. <u>Anton and Pam</u> spot a coral reef beneath the water.

16. <u>The reef</u> has brightly colored fish around it.

17. <u>The skillful diver</u> slips into the water.

18. <u>A jellyfish</u> is there.

19. <u>Anton's sister</u> shouts a warning.

20. <u>Anton</u> swims out of the way.

21. <u>The diver</u> breathes a sigh of relief.

22. <u>Soldierfish</u> swim by.

23. <u>Anton</u> photographs the rose-colored fish.

24. <u>Anton's talent</u> is well known.

25. Tomorrow <u>Pam and Anton</u> will photograph fish together.

ADDITIONAL PRACTICE
Object Pronouns

A. Write the object pronouns in these sentences.

Example:

Carola's father took her to the amusement park.
her

1. Carola led him over to the speedway.

2. "This is the ride for me!" Carola said.

3. Carola's father bought two tickets for them.

4. She gave them to the ride operator.

5. "Put us in the fastest car, please," Carola said to the operator.

6. "Give us the slowest car," Carola's father said.

7. The operator smiled at them.

8. "Promise me you will not break the sound barrier," said the operator to Carola.

9. He put them into a fast red sports car.

10. Carola's father drove it around the track swiftly but safely.

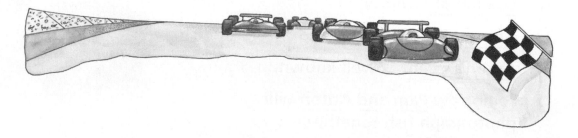

B. Revise each sentence. Replace the underlined word or words with an object pronoun.

Example:

Cathy and I saw <u>the tortoises</u> first.
them

11. I have been to <u>this beach</u> before.

12. I have never seen <u>a tortoise</u> here.

13. They live with <u>other tortoises</u>.

14. Many tortoises share <u>one area</u>.

15. They dig <u>tunnels</u>.

16. Look for <u>a pile of dirt</u> at the tunnel's mouth.

17. A tortoise dug <u>another tunnel</u> with its feet.

18. Cathy went to tell <u>Ranger Leo</u> the news.

19. Ranger Leo came back with <u>Cathy</u>.

20. We counted <u>tortoises</u> for six hours.

21. We carefully arranged <u>our cameras</u>.

22. I asked permission from <u>Ranger Leo</u> first.

23. He gave permission to <u>this photographer</u>.

24. We will develop <u>the photos</u> tomorrow morning.

ADDITIONAL PRACTICE
Adjectives

A. Write the adjective or adjectives in each sentence. Do not include *a, an,* or *the.*

Example:

A long time ago, people believed the earth was flat.
long, flat

1. Magellan was a brave captain.

2. He commanded a fleet of five ships.

3. There were difficult problems.

4. Many crewmen would not follow orders.

5. A fierce storm destroyed one ship.

6. There wasn't enough food.

7. The unhappy crew stopped for food and water in the Philippines.

8. The sailors were hungry and thirsty.

9. One ship returned home to Spain.

10. The journey proved that the earth is round.

Writing Application Imagine a terrible storm. Use adjectives to write sentences about the sounds, sights, and smells you would experience in such a storm.

B. Write the adjective in each sentence. Do not include *a, an,* or *the.* Also write the noun the adjective describes.

Example:

A lively goat jumped from rock to rock.
lively, goat

11. The goat made four jumps in a row.

12. Lucy took pictures of the graceful animal.

13. The goat went behind a huge boulder.

14. Lucy put a new roll of film into the camera.

15. She watched for sudden movements on the mountainside.

16. Three goats appeared on the trail.

17. Lucy admired their white coats.

18. She focused her small camera.

19. She took five pictures quickly.

20. The suspicious goats hopped away from Lucy.

21. They made long shadows on the rocks.

22. The red sun set behind the mountains.

23. Lucy buttoned her heavy coat.

24. She happily began the long hike down the trail.

ADDITIONAL PRACTICE

Adjectives That Tell *How Many*

A. Write each adjective that tells how many. Some adjectives are made up of two words.

Example:

The distance from Earth to Mars is about fifty million miles.
fifty million

1. Several astronauts climb aboard the spacecraft.

2. One billion people watch the launch on TV.

3. Everyone counts out loud during the final ten seconds.

4. Three powerful rockets blast the crew into space.

5. The journey to Mars takes many months.

6. The crew members eat at least two meals a day.

7. They sleep for seven hours every night.

8. Finally, five astronauts land on Mars.

9. The temperature is one hundred degrees below zero!

B. Revise these sentences. Replace each blank with an adjective that tells how many.

Example:

I will have ____ partners.
three

10. I will become a famous explorer when I am ____ years old.

11. We will travel ____ miles.

12. Our journey will last ____ days.

13. We will pack ____ pounds of food.

14. I will take ____ pairs of shoes.

15. On the hottest day, the temperature will be ____ degrees.

16. On the coldest day, the temperature will be ____ degrees below zero.

17. We will check our map ____ times.

18. We will cook ____ meals.

19. We will use ____ feet of rope.

20. We will discover ____ kinds of plants.

21. We will take photographs of ____ rare animals.

22. We will find a treasure worth ____ dollars.

23. Our pictures will be on the covers of ____ magazines.

ADDITIONAL PRACTICE
Adjectives That Tell *What Kind*

A. List each adjective that tells what kind.

Example:

I wrote a long letter to my sister.
long

1. It tells about an interesting experience I am having.
2. I'm learning new things every day in camp.
3. The unit is called the Green Giants.
4. We painted a large sign with the name.
5. You would have a great time here.
6. We helped build a wooden path for the trail.
7. The unit found a hidden nest.
8. Tiny rabbits were in it.
9. We were a silent group of observers.
10. Look in the envelope for a funny souvenir.

Writing Application Everyone has places that are special to him or her. Think about a place that is special to you. Write a paragraph describing how the place looks, smells, and sounds. Underline the adjectives that tell *what kind*.

B. Write the adjective in each sentence that tells what kind. Also, write the noun that it describes.

Example:

Light rain falls on the plains.
light, rain

11. The tall grasses bend in the wind.

12. The rain moistens the dry earth.

13. Umaru drives along a narrow road.

14. He is headed for market in the busy city.

15. The truck carries heavy sacks of grain.

16. A large piece of canvas keeps them dry.

17. Umaru cannot sell wet grain.

18. He worries about the dark clouds.

19. Suddenly a sharp stone punctures a tire!

20. He must change the flat tire.

21. Umaru tries to turn the rusty bolts.

22. It is hard to remove the damaged tire.

23. Then he remembers the red can he bought at the store.

24. Umaru sprays its special mixture into the tire.

25. Umaru's difficult problem is solved!

ADDITIONAL PRACTICE
Articles

A. Write the articles in these sentences.

Example:

A huge bass leaps out of the water.
A, the

1. Chesapeake Bay is home to a great many creatures.

2. In the 1960s, the bay was becoming polluted.

3. Chesapeake Bay is now a cleaner and safer place for wild creatures.

4. An otter runs along the shore.

5. An eagle glides across the sky.

6. An old turtle dives off a log.

7. A beautiful swan spreads its wings.

8. Oysters live on the rocky floor of the bay.

9. An osprey dives into the water.

10. A fish is the osprey's target.

B. Write an article that would fit well in each sentence.

Example:

Loggerhead turtles are ____ endangered species.

an

11. ____ female turtle laid her eggs last night.

12. First, she dug ____ hole in ____ sand.

13. Then, she laid her eggs in ____ hole.

14. She covered ____ eggs with sand.

15. ____ female turtle does not stay at the nest.

16. It is against ____ law to disturb these nests.

17. However, Alfredo is ____ wildlife professional.

18. He alone may take ____ eggs.

19. Alfredo digs in ____ sand and finds ____ nest!

20. He puts ____ eggs into ____ ice chest.

21. Then he fills ____ chest with wet sand.

ADDITIONAL PRACTICE
Adjectives That Compare: *-er, -est*

A. Read the sentences. Write each adjective that compares two things. There are four.

Example:

This crocodile is longer than that one.
longer

1. Alligators have rounder snouts than crocodiles.

2. Crocodiles' eggs are bigger than hens' eggs.

3. The crocodile is one of the largest of all reptiles.

4. It is faster than an alligator.

5. The saltwater crocodile is larger than an alligator.

B. Write each adjective that compares more than two things. There are four.

Example:

The goby is one of the smallest of all fish.
smallest

6. The giraffe is the tallest mammal of all.

7. The African elephant is larger than the Asian elephant.

8. The cheetah is the fastest land animal.

9. Dogs are the easiest mammals to train.

10. Bears are the strongest mammals.

C. Revise each sentence. Change the word in parentheses ( ) to its correct form.

Example:

Otters are the (cute) animals of all in the zoo.
cutest

11. This otter is (fast) than the other one.

12. A mongoose's strike is (quick) than a snake's.

13. Are owls the (wise) of all birds?

14. That tortoise is (old) than any other animal here.

15. Its shell is (thick) than a turtle's.

16. Which of all the snakes is the (long)?

17. The new snake house is (large) than the old one.

18. Which bear has the (thick) fur of all the bears?

19. Penguins live in the (cold) of all places on Earth.

20. House cats have the (soft) fur of all.

21. Are chicken eggs (small) than ostrich eggs?

22. Is the shrew the (small) mammal in all the world?

ADDITIONAL PRACTICE

Adjectives That Compare: *More, Most*

A. Read the sentences. Write only the adjectives that compare two things.

Example:

Tropical fish are more colorful than Arctic fish.
more colorful

1. Salmon are more rapid swimmers than perch.

2. Great white sharks are more dangerous to swimmers than nurse sharks.

3. Guppies are the most popular fish.

4. Catfish are more common than sharks.

5. The grass carp is more useful than many other fish because it eats weeds.

B. Write only the adjectives that compare more than two things.

6. Rays have the most unusual shape of any fish.

7. The electric eel produces the most powerful electric charge of any creature.

8. An eel is more difficult to hold than a trout.

9. Tuna may be the most common fish we eat.

10. Is fish the most healthy meat there is?

C. Complete each sentence. Write *more* or *most* to make a correct comparison.

Example:

Amphibians may be the ____ interesting creatures in the world.
most

11. The salamander is the ____ unusual amphibian. It breathes through its skin.

12. Are frogs ____ unusual than salamanders?

13. Do frogs have the ____ accurate tongues for catching insects?

14. A chameleon's tongue is ____ accurate than a frog's.

15. The frogs that glide through the air are the ____ amazing of all.

16. Frogs can be ____ colorful than many other creatures.

17. One small red frog is the ____ poisonous creature on earth.

18. Chameleons are ____ amazing than frogs because they can change color.

19. Frogs have ____ beautiful voices than any other animal.

20. Some think a frog's voice is ____ bothersome than any other animal's voice.

ADDITIONAL PRACTICE
Verbs

A. Read the sentences. Write the verb used in each one.

Example:

Mrs. Stein makes costumes for actors in plays.
makes

1. Before the school play, Mrs. Stein visits our class.

2. Each child drew a picture of a costume.

3. Last year, Ling painted a picture of a bumblebee.

4. The bumblebee looked very busy!

5. Mrs. Stein unrolled some yellow felt.

6. She and Ling cut two ovals from the cloth.

7. Mrs. Stein sewed the ovals together.

8. Ling attached black paper for stripes.

9. Two pieces of plastic formed the wings.

10. Ling buzzed through the room in her bee costume.

B. Read each pair of sentences. In the blank, write a verb that makes sense.

Example:

Frogs are amphibians. They ____ both on land and in water.
live

11. **Elkin's yard has a garden and a creek. He ____ outside all day.**

12. **The garden needs water to grow. Elkin ____ the garden.**

13. **Elkin's grandfather planted flowers there. They ____ quickly.**

14. **Frogs in the creek croak loudly. Elkin ____ them in the evening.**

15. **Tadpoles are young frogs. They ____ in the water, just like fish.**

16. **One day Elkin found a rabbit's nest. The mother ____ in front of him.**

17. **Elkin wondered how many baby rabbits were in the nest. He ____ eight of them.**

18. **Elkin knew the mother would come right back. He ____ away from the nest.**

ADDITIONAL PRACTICE
Action Verbs

A. Read each sentence. Write the action verb.

Example:

Travelers in Africa often see ostriches.
see

1. Ostriches run very fast.
2. They jump high, too.
3. They kick with their strong legs.
4. Lions chase ostriches.
5. The ostriches usually escape.
6. These tall birds build nests on the sand.
7. First, the male ostrich digs a hole.
8. Then a female lays several large eggs.
9. The male warms the eggs with his body.
10. The chicks hatch after about forty-five days.

B. Read each sentence. In the blank, write an action verb that makes sense.

Example:

Anteaters ____ ants with their tongues.
catch

11. Beavers ____ dams in streams.

12. Bats ____ at night.

13. Frogs ____ loudly.

14. Roosters ____ noisily in the morning.

15. Monkeys ____ from branch to branch in the tall trees.

16. Cheetahs ____ very fast.

17. Kangaroos ____ high and far.

18. Some whales ____ thousands of miles across the ocean.

19. Woodpeckers ____ holes in trees.

20. Squirrels ____ nuts in the ground.

21. Pandas ____ bamboo and many other plants.

22. Owls ____ after mice.

23. Skunks ____ a bad smell when they are attacked.

24. Lizards ____ quietly on rocks in the sun.

ADDITIONAL PRACTICE
Main Verbs

A. Write the main verb used in each sentence.

Example:

Caleb and Maya have packed their equipment.
packed

1. Maya has planned this day for months.

2. She and Caleb have traveled to the sea.

3. Caleb had collected more than two hundred different shells.

4. He has placed them all in boxes.

5. He has searched the whole reef.

6. They have used special equipment for this search.

7. Maya has stored her shells in a sack.

8. She has picked the best ones.

9. Maya has adjusted her snorkel.

10. She had cleaned it carefully.

Writing Application Talk with a partner about some activities your class has done. Then write four to six sentences about the activities, using a main verb and a helping verb in each sentence.

B. Write the verbs used in each sentence. Underline the main verb.

Example:

David has arrived at Uncle Gary's ranch.
has <u>arrived</u>

11. David had visited him there three times before.

12. He had arrived by jet.

13. They have unpacked David's things.

14. Uncle Gary has raised llamas on his ranch for eight years.

15. They have helped him in many ways.

16. Uncle Gary has traded their wool for equipment.

17. The llamas have provided transportation, too.

18. David has gone on a camping trip.

19. The llamas have walked this way before.

20. They have enjoyed the hike.

21. David and Uncle Gary have cooked a meal.

22. They have finished eating now.

ADDITIONAL PRACTICE
Helping Verbs

A. Write the helping verb used in each sentence.

Example:

We have watched a sunrise today.
have

1. I have enjoyed the bright colors of dawn.

2. My sister Ann has joined me.

3. She had baked muffins for breakfast.

4. We have hiked to the top of a mountain.

5. Pink streaks of light have filled the sky.

6. Geese had honked at each other for hours earlier.

7. Ann and I have worked together outside before.

8. We have looked at the whole countryside.

9. Ann has finished her painting of the geese.

10. I have framed mine.

Writing Application Everyone enjoys some kinds of games and sports. Think about some games you have played. Write a few sentences about one of the games. Use helping verbs and main verbs in your sentences.

B. Write the verbs used in each sentence. Underline the helping verb.

Example:

The ape has moved swiftly through the treetops.

<u>has</u> moved

11. These apes have lived in tropical forests for thousands of years.

12. My camera has recorded their graceful motions.

13. One of them had slipped.

14. Has it injured its leg?

15. No, it has climbed back up the tree.

16. Another ape had helped it.

17. One ape has provided food for its neighbor.

18. They have liked their view from the treetops.

19. I have used all my film.

20. We had learned much from this project.

ADDITIONAL PRACTICE

Present-tense Verbs

A. Read each sentence. Write the present-tense form of the verb shown in parentheses ( ).

Example:

My cat (arched/arches) his back.
arches

1. I (look/looked) at him.

2. He (sees/saw) something.

3. I (thought/think) it is a rope.

4. The rope (surprised/surprises) me.

5. It (moves/moved) by itself.

6. I (call/called) my mom.

7. She (knew/knows) about snakes.

8. This breed (hunted/hunts) only mice.

9. Mom (wraps/wrapped) it in a towel.

10. She (put/puts) it back outside.

B. Revise each sentence. Change the underlined verb so it tells about the present.

Example:

The chickens walked out of the henhouse.
The chickens walk out of the henhouse.

11. The chickens clucked a hello.

12. They stretched their wings.

13. Two hens pecked at some grain.

14. A chicken gobbled up a slug.

15. The puppy jumped up and down.

16. He barked loudly at the chickens.

17. The chickens scattered in the yard.

18. The farm owner greeted the chickens.

19. She tossed them some broccoli and squash.

20. They nibbled the vegetables happily.

21. A large hen scratched at the dirt in the yard.

22. A chick followed her.

23. Two other chickens wandered over.

24. A little hen discovered some bugs.

25. She shared the bugs with the other hens.

practice

ADDITIONAL PRACTICE

Past-tense Verbs

A. Read the sentences. Write each past-tense verb.

Example:

Shana created a number trick for her math project.
created

1. First, she sketched a triangle on a sheet of paper.

2. Then, she traced a circle at each corner of the triangle.

3. Next, she added a circle in the middle of each side.

4. Shana jotted a number from 1 to 6 inside each circle.

5. The three numbers on each side of the triangle totaled 12.

6. Tim checked Shana's addition carefully.

7. Shana demonstrated her number trick to the class.

8. Some students solved the puzzle quickly.

9. Shana's teacher praised her project.

10. Later, some other students invented their own number tricks.

B. Revise each sentence. Change the verb in parentheses ( ) to its past-tense form.

Example:

Rita (construct) a puzzle yesterday.
constructed

11. First, she (sketch) a triangle on a piece of paper.

12. Next, she (mark) five steps on each side.

13. Then, she (show) a step at the top.

14. She (reproduce) the drawing onto a block of wood.

15. Her father quickly (saw) the wood.

16. Rita (move) the finished puzzle.

17. She (place) a red marker on each step on the right side.

18. She (arrange) a blue marker on each step on the left side.

19. Rita (complete) the puzzle on her first try!

20. Then, she (hand) the puzzle to her father.

21. After an hour, Rita's dad (ask) for her help.

ADDITIONAL PRACTICE
Irregular Verbs

A. Read each sentence. Choose the correct form of the verb in parentheses ( ).

Example:

We (drove/driven) to a museum by the sea.
drove

1. It (gave/given) me a new idea for a hobby.

2. Mom (drove/driven) me to the supermarket.

3. "We have (eaten/ate) dinner already," she said.

4. We (went/goes) anyway.

5. I had (gone/went) into the store.

6. I (came/comes) out with an empty milk jug.

7. We (drove/drives) home.

8. I have (gave/given) the model I made to my mom.

9. "How (done/did) you get a model ship inside this small jug?" she asked.

10. "I have (do/done) the impossible," I grinned.

Writing Application Make a chart. List six irregular verbs in the left column. In the right column, write one sentence with each verb.

B. Revise these sentences. Change the underlined present-tense verbs to the correct form of the past-tense verb.

Example:

I <u>do</u> research for my report yesterday.
did

11. I have <u>eat</u> many foods.

12. I thought I had <u>do</u> all my research.

13. Our dog Rusty <u>come</u> into the kitchen.

14. I <u>give</u> him a delicious dog biscuit.

15. "Rusty, what <u>do</u> you think of it?" I asked.

16. He <u>go</u> to the food cabinet.

17. "I have just <u>give</u> you the last one," I said.

18. I had <u>go</u> into the garage to speak to my dad.

19. A minute later, Dad <u>drive</u> me to the store.

20. When I had <u>comes</u> out, I had a present for Rusty.

21. He <u>eat</u> and <u>eat</u> those special treats.

ADDITIONAL PRACTICE
More Irregular Verbs

A. Read each sentence. Change the verb in parentheses ( ) to its correct form.

Example:

I once (see) tall statues in a place called Easter Island.
saw

1. Last year a plane (take) us to visit this faraway place.
2. Our tour guide has (say) these statues are a mystery.
3. Scientists had (think) they were carved by local island people.
4. Yesterday the tour bus (ride) from place to place.
5. A few times we got off the bus and (run) around.
6. I (see) statues everywhere I looked.
7. Each one's face (have) a serious look.
8. I have (take) many photographs.
9. Back then, I had (think) they would make nice postcards.
10. I have not (have) them developed yet.

B. Read each sentence. Choose the verb in parentheses ( ) that is correct.

Example:

Lyle (taken/took) a trip to Philadelphia last weekend.

took

11. He (ride/rode) in the front seat next to his dad.

12. He (have/had) his pet parrot in the back seat.

13. Every time the parrot (saw/seen) something it liked, it squawked.

14. Lyle and his dad (thought/thinks) for a while.

15. Then Lyle's dad (have/had) a good idea.

16. "Teach it to say hello," he (say/said).

17. As they (ridden/rode) along, Lyle taught the parrot the word *hello*.

18. It (took/taken) a few hours.

19. Lyle had almost (run/ran) out of hope.

20. Suddenly, the parrot (seen/saw) another bird.

21. "Hello! Hello!" it (say/said).

22. Lyle was glad he had (taken/took) his father's advice.

ADDITIONAL PRACTICE
The Verb *Be*

A. Write the form of the verb *be* used in each sentence.

Example:

Yesterday the bus was on time.
was

1. Today the bus is late.

2. The streets were noisy by 8 o'clock yesterday morning.

3. From my window I see the streets are quiet.

4. I am already late for school.

5. My friends are probably all there by now.

6. The bus driver is usually nice.

7. Why is everything so odd today?

8. Yesterday was Friday, not Thursday!

9. Today is not a school day!

10. The bus and I are not late.

Writing Application Imagine that one day everyone comes to school on the weekend for a special project. Write about how you and other students feel and what you do. Use the verb *be* correctly.

B. Read each sentence. Write a form of the verb *be* that correctly completes each sentence.

Example:

Today my boots ____ in the closet.
are

11. Today ____ December 20.

12. Today's weather ____ warm.

13. There ____ many hours of daylight left.

14. Some people ____ at the beach.

15. We ____ at a picnic all day yesterday.

16. December ____ a cold month.

17. Last December, snow ____ on the ground.

18. The sky ____ gray this time last year.

19. Today the sky ____ blue.

20. Last year the only kangaroos near us ____ in a warm room at the zoo.

21. Today some kangaroos ____ in the field across from our home.

22. Why ____ December so different this year?

23. We ____ in Australia!

ADDITIONAL PRACTICE
Adverbs

A. Write the adverb used in each sentence.

Example:

Teresa often visits her grandmother in Hawaii.
often

1. Teresa arrived at the Hilo airport yesterday.

2. Grandma NeNe greeted Teresa warmly.

3. Now the two of them are making flower necklaces.

4. Teresa runs ahead to gather pink lokelani flowers.

5. Grandma NeNe swiftly threads a curved needle with string.

6. Teresa has already lined up the flowers.

7. Teresa carefully pokes the needle through each flower.

8. Grandma NeNe expertly knots the ends of the string.

9. Teresa proudly wears the beautiful necklace.

10. Grandma NeNe stands nearby.

Writing Application Everyone has special talents and skills. Think about something you do well. Write a few sentences about how you do it, using adverbs in your sentences.

B. Revise each sentence. Replace the underlined adverb with another adverb of your choice.

Example:

Marco's mother <u>usually</u> practices the piano.
Marco's mother <u>often</u> practices the piano.

11. Marco <u>eagerly</u> helps his mother.

12. He <u>carefully</u> turns the pages of her music book.

13. Marco's mother plays <u>skillfully</u>.

14. <u>Sometimes</u> she stops, though.

15. Marco <u>immediately</u> checks the music book.

16. He finds the next notes <u>quickly</u>.

17. <u>Then</u> he locates the correct piano keys.

18. He <u>lightly</u> touches each key.

19. Marco and his mother <u>always</u> laugh at mistakes.

20. They sing the words of a song <u>cheerfully</u>.

21. Marco looks <u>outside</u> and smiles.

22. A crowd has gathered <u>nearby</u>.

ADDITIONAL PRACTICE
To, Too, Two

A. Read each sentence. Write *to, too,* or *two.*

Example:

Last winter Uma and her mother went ____ Norway.
to

1. They visited their ____ friends, Marta and Bjorn.

2. They flew ____ a village north of the Arctic Circle.

3. They arrived in a village at ____ o'clock in the afternoon.

4. The stars were out, and the moon was rising, ____.

5. Marta said the sun would not rise again for ____ more weeks.

6. Bjorn and Marta invited their guests ____ a masked ball.

7. On the day of the first sunrise, Bjorn gave a party mask ____ Uma.

8. Marta gave her a mask, ____.

9. Uma showed one of her masks ____ her mother.

10. The four friends hurried ____ the center of town.

Writing Application Make a poster telling people to visit your city or town. Use the words *to, too,* and *two.*

B. Proofread each sentence, and rewrite it correctly.

Example:

I will give a journal too Lisa for her birthday.
I will give a journal to Lisa for her birthday.

11. I will give her a nice pen, two.

12. Those too things will be a good present.

13. Lisa gave a journal too me last year.

14. I write a page or to in it every day.

15. I took it two my aunt's home this summer.

16. She keeps a journal, to.

17. She read parts of her old journal too me.

18. One part told about her trip two Jamaica.

19. She stayed for to months.

20. My aunt is a good writer and a good cook, two.

21. She gave one of her favorite recipes too me.

22. I cooked it and ate it, to.

23. The too of us enjoyed being together.

24. Soon I will go too Lisa's party.

25. I will walk the to blocks two her house.

ADDITIONAL PRACTICE
Your, You're

A. Read the sentences. Write *your* or *you're* to complete each sentence.

Example:

Wouldn't it be great if you and ____ friends could make all the rules for a day?
your

1. If ____ in Turkey on April 23, you will enjoy Children's Day there.

2. You and ____ classmates might be elected to run the government.

3. All the laws would be ____ responsibility for one day.

4. Would you ask ____ classmates to vote for you on Children's Day?

5. On Children's Day ____ transportation is free.

6. On that day ____ allowed into the movies for free.

7. ____ stomach might ache from eating too much.

8. If ____ visiting from another country, you can take part in a parade.

9. Perhaps ____ family will have a chance to visit Turkey someday.

10. ____ likely to remember ____ visit to Turkey.

B. Read the sentences. Write the word in parentheses ( ) that completes each sentence correctly.

Example:

"(Your/You're) up next, Wei," the coach said.
You're

11. "Here's (your/you're) favorite bat," said Roger.

12. "I know (your/you're) going to get a hit," he said.

13. "Keep (your/you're) eye on the ball," the coach yelled.

14. "(Your/You're) going to get a hit," Wei told himself.

15. "I can hit (your/you're) fastball," Wei thought.

16. "(Your/You're) not going to get me out!" Wei said silently.

17. "I knew I could hit (your/you're) fastball!" Wei said as he smacked the ball hard.

18. "(Your/You're) the champ," the catcher said to Wei as he scored the winning run.

ADDITIONAL PRACTICE

Its, It's

A. Read each sentence. Decide whether *its* or *it's* would be correct in the blank.

Example:

____ really raining hard!

It's

1. ____ a good thing I remembered my umbrella today!

2. I will take my umbrella out of ____ case.

3. The case won't open because ____ snap is stuck.

4. ____ hard to open a snap when your hands are wet.

5. Now ____ time for me to open my umbrella!

6. ____ going to feel good to be protected from the rain!

7. I'm trying to open my umbrella, but ____ not working.

8. ____ pole is bent.

9. There! I've fixed my umbrella, and ____ open at last!

10. Now ____ not raining anymore.

Writing Application Different people like different kinds of weather. What kind of weather do you like? Write three sentences about it. Be sure to use *its* and *it's* correctly.

B. Proofread each sentence, and write it correctly. Correct the spelling or capitalization of each underlined word.

Example:

<u>its</u> my turn to use the computer!
It's my turn to use the computer!

11. A computer stores information in <u>it's</u> memory.

12. <u>its</u> important to know how much memory your computer has.

13. This computer game is good because <u>its</u> an educational game.

14. You cannot play this game on your computer because <u>it's</u> memory is too small.

15. <u>it's</u> time to add some memory to your computer!

16. Mom says <u>its</u> easy to add memory to a computer.

17. If you put this chip into your computer, you will increase the size of <u>it's</u> memory.

18. Let's test your computer to see if <u>Its</u> new memory chip is working.

19. Great! <u>Its</u> working perfectly!

20. I like this game because <u>it's</u> pictures are colorful!

ADDITIONAL PRACTICE

Their, There, They're

A. Read each sentence. Decide whether *their, there,* or *they're* is correct, and write the missing word.

Example:

Our grandparents want us to know more about ____ lives.
their

1. ____ writing a book for us.

2. The book is a history of ____ lives.

3. They keep the book at ____ house.

4. We go over ____ for dinner on Sundays.

5. Grandma and Grandpa have put ____ old photographs in the book.

6. ____ very interesting to look at.

7. ____ is my favorite picture of Grandma.

8. I wish I had been with them ____ at the Seattle World's Fair.

9. ____ both great storytellers.

10. Sometimes they share ____ memories with us before they write them.

B. Proofread each sentence, and write it correctly. Correct the spelling of each underlined word.

Example:

Elephants are famous for <u>there</u> good memory.
Elephants are famous for their good memory.

11. Elephants are useful because of <u>there</u> strength and intelligence.

12. <u>Theyre</u> used as work animals in Thailand.

13. They haul logs through the forest <u>their</u>.

14. It's not easy to prove how good <u>there</u> memory really is.

15. <u>their</u> able to remember many commands.

16. Dogs use <u>they're</u> memory, too.

17. They remember the scent of <u>there</u> owners.

18. <u>Their</u> able to remember where home is.

19. Some dogs find <u>there</u> way back home from hundreds of miles away.

20. No one is sure how <u>their</u> able to do this.

21. Dolphins have large brains for <u>they're</u> body size.

22. <u>Their</u> very intelligent animals.

23. <u>They're</u> language is made up of clicks, squeaks, and whistles.

ADDITIONAL PRACTICE

Comma After Introductory Words

A. Write each sentence. Add a comma after the introductory word.

Example:

"Well it's time to open the photo album," said Ben.
"Well, it's time to open the photo album," said Ben.

1. "Yes I have been looking forward to this," said Joni.

2. "Well do you recognize that person?" said Ben.

3. "No I don't," Noli replied.

4. "Yes that is my cousin Jonny," Max replied.

5. "Well have you ever met him, Joni?"

6. "Well I must have met him, but I don't remember him," she replied as she looked at the photos.

7. "Yes let's look at the photos of our trip to New York," Ben said.

8. "No I would rather see the photos of our visit to the Grand Canyon," Max said.

Writing Application What steps do you follow to make your favorite sandwich? Write a paragraph telling how to make the sandwich. Use commas after the words *First*, *Next*, and *Finally*.

B. Read each sentence. Write an introductory word that makes sense in the blank. Remember to add a comma.

Example:

"____ I remember our visit to Finland," said Ruth. "Do you remember it, Bela?"
Yes,

9. "____ I do," said Bela. "We went with Grandma in 1992."

10. "____ we went in 1993," said Ruth. "We left on Valentine's Day."

11. "____ we left on St. Patrick's Day. That's why you wore a green dress!"

12. "____ I think you're wrong," Ruth replied. "I'm sure I wore a red dress because it was Valentine's Day!"

13. "____ here is a picture of us getting on the plane in Ohio," said Bela.

14. "____ this is a picture of us getting on the plane in Helsinki," said Ruth.

15. "____ you're wrong, Ruth," said Bela. "It must be Cleveland because you're wearing a green dress!"

16. "____ you wouldn't remember that," said Bela.

17. "____ I would. I have a very good memory."

ADDITIONAL PRACTICE
Series Comma

A. Revise each sentence by adding commas where they belong.

Example:

Istanbul is a large beautiful and ancient city.
Istanbul is a large, beautiful, and ancient city.

1. My sister my parents and my grandparents all went to see the palace there.

2. In the palace we saw a throne room a swimming pool and some guest rooms.

3. Our tour guide spoke French German and English.

4. The palace rooms were decorated with stones rugs and jewels.

5. People came long ago from India China and Europe to bring the sultan gifts.

6. We were hot tired and hungry after the tour.

7. At lunch we had lamb grapes and baklava.

8. Then we went to the market, which was busy loud and colorful.

9. The apricots figs and dates all looked delicious.

10. That evening we watched boats barges and ferries glide past the city.

B. Proofread each sentence, and rewrite it correctly. Put commas in the correct places. Take out any commas that do not belong.

Example:

My mother my father and, I were eating dinner.
My mother, my father, and I were eating dinner.

11. We were having lamb chops, mashed potatoes and, peas.

12. Lightning flashed thunder crashed, and rain began falling.

13. The wind, whistled howled and moaned.

14. Thunder rumbled, crashed and boomed.

15. The windows rattled, the screen door banged, and, the lights went out.

16. Lightning jumped leaped and danced across the, sky.

17. I shivered moaned, and cried.

18. The house, was damp dark and scary.

19. My mother brought out, a flashlight a candle and matches.

20. Mom Dad and, I did not feel like eating.

21. We told jokes played games and sang, songs.